Easter
Coloring Book

Adult Colouring Books

Aryla Publishing 2018

978 1 912675 01 2

www.arylapublishing.com

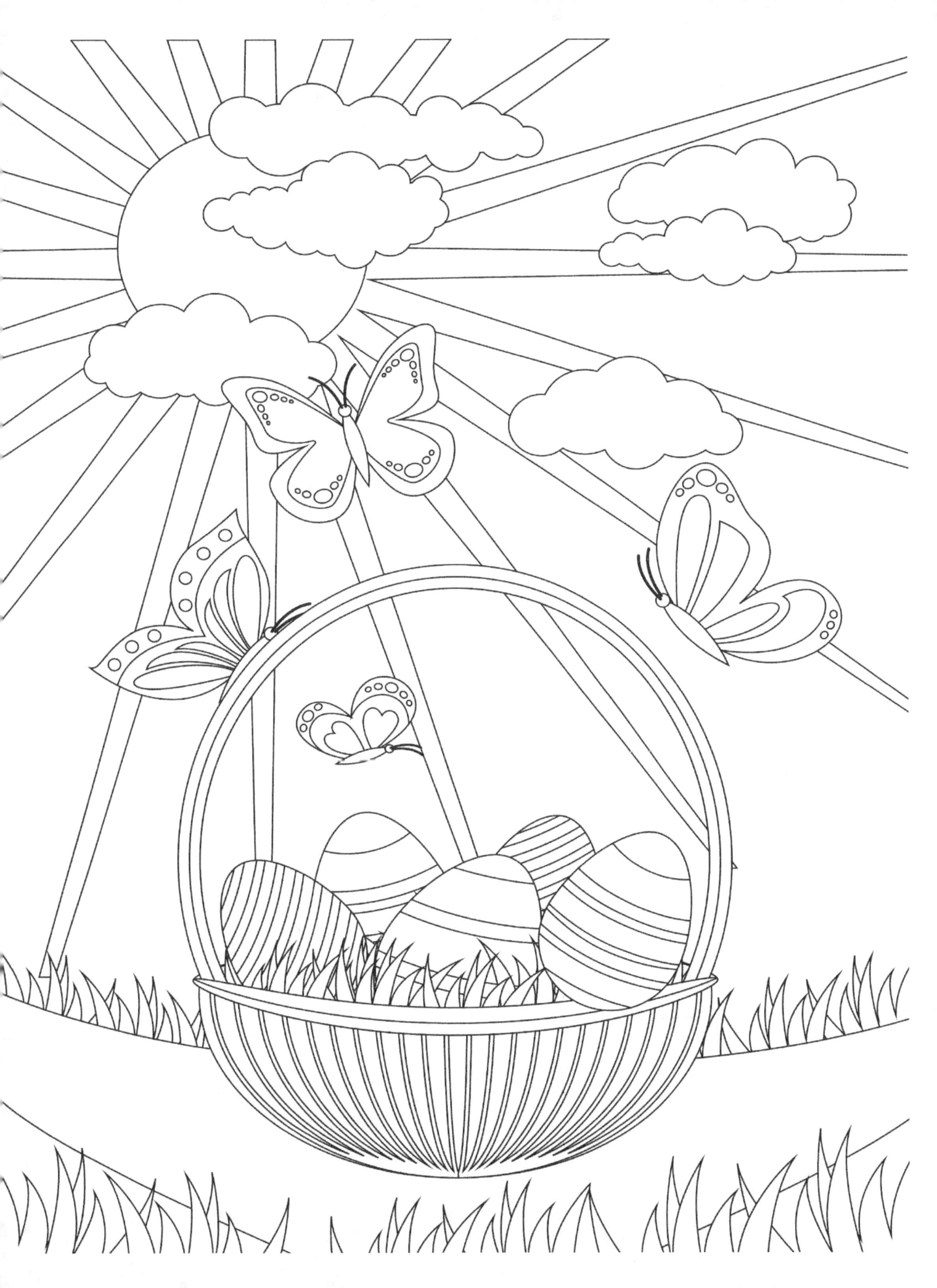

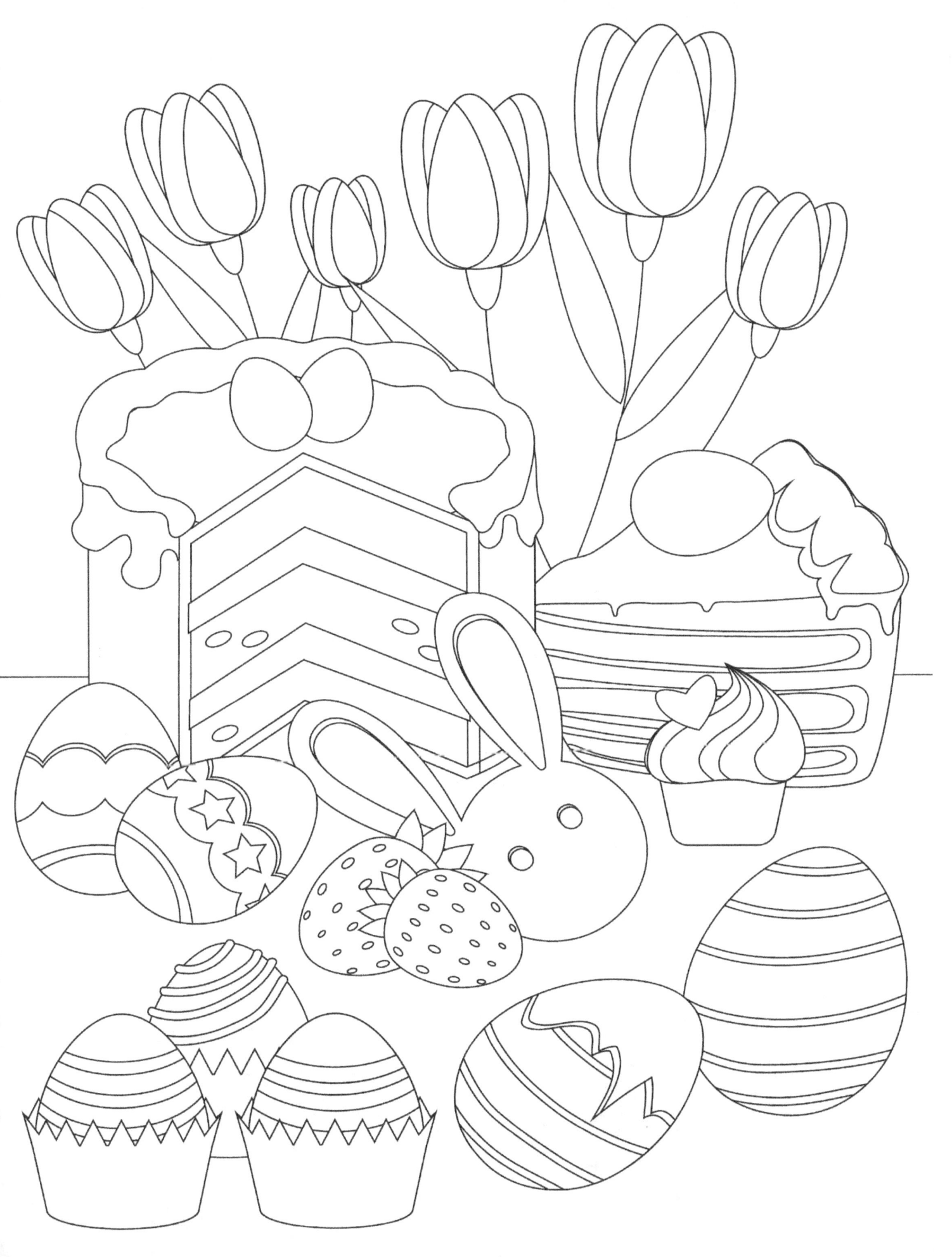

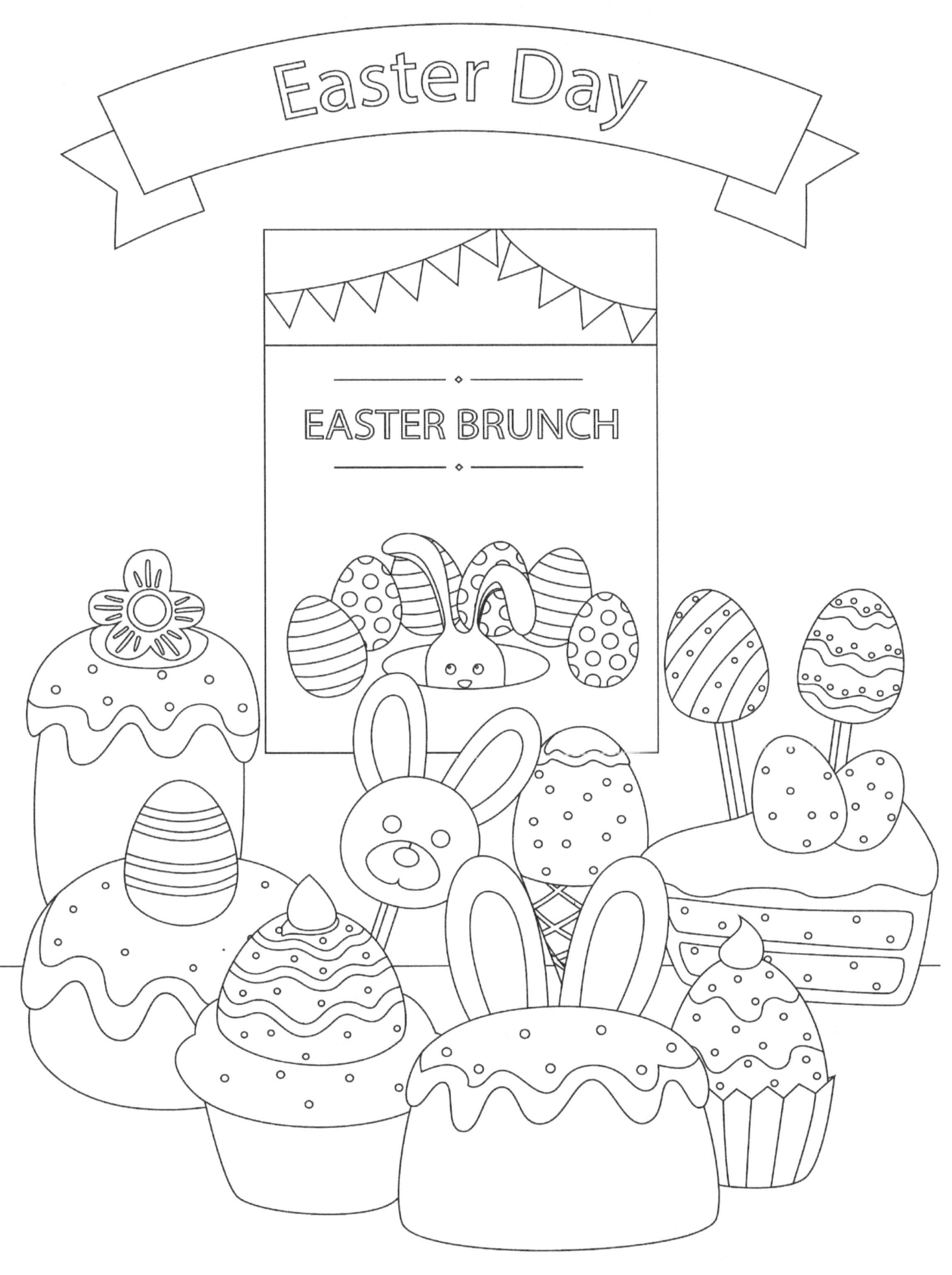

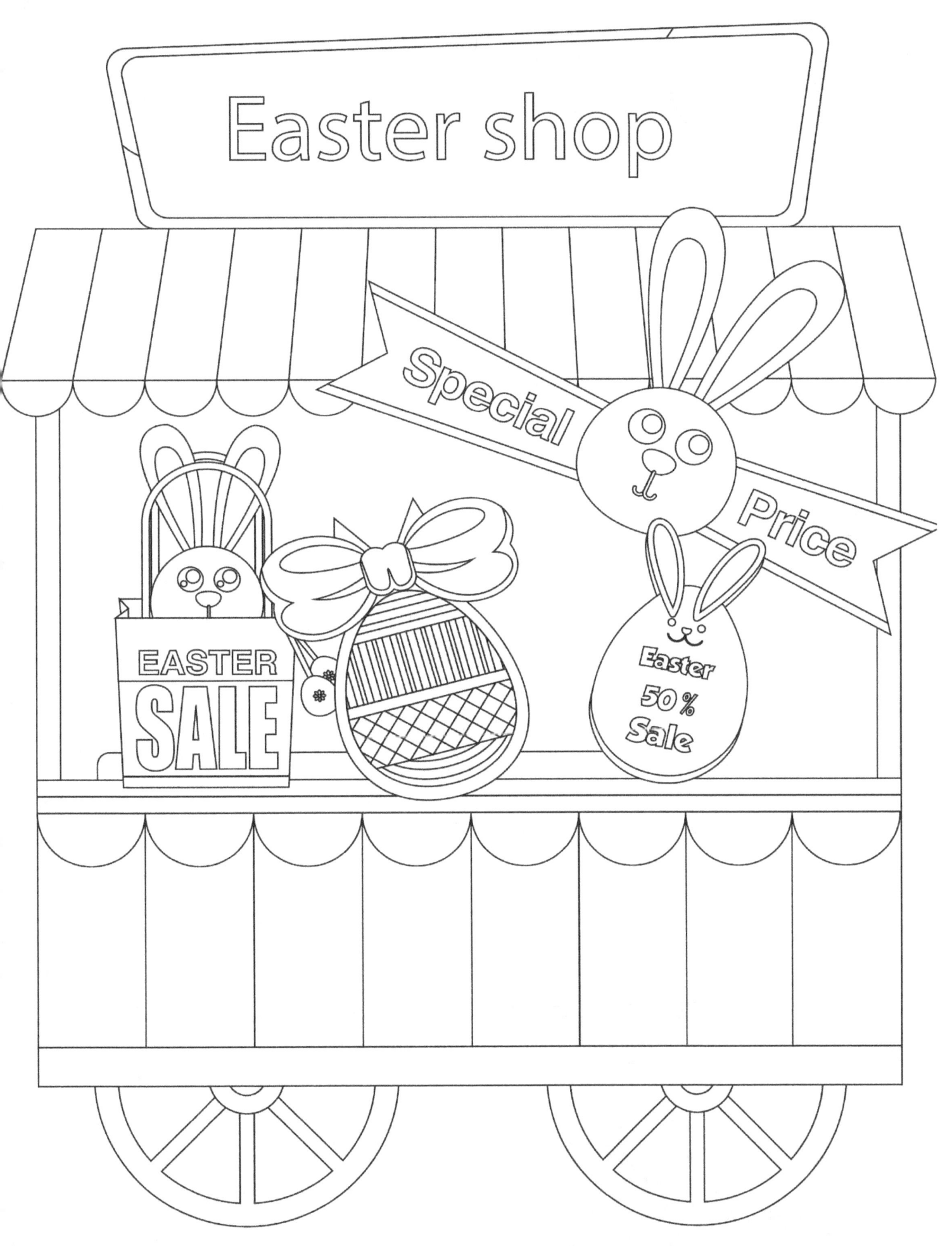

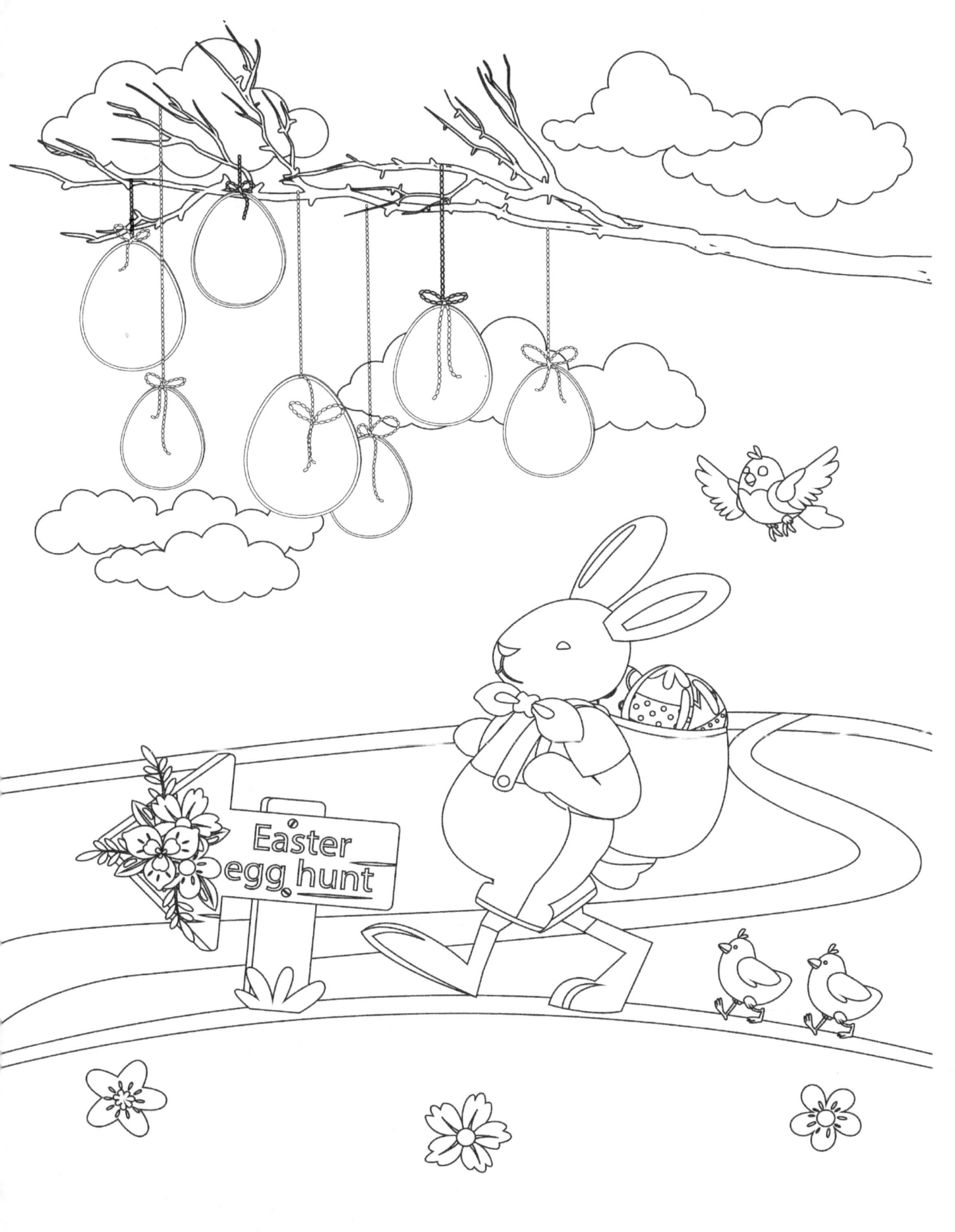

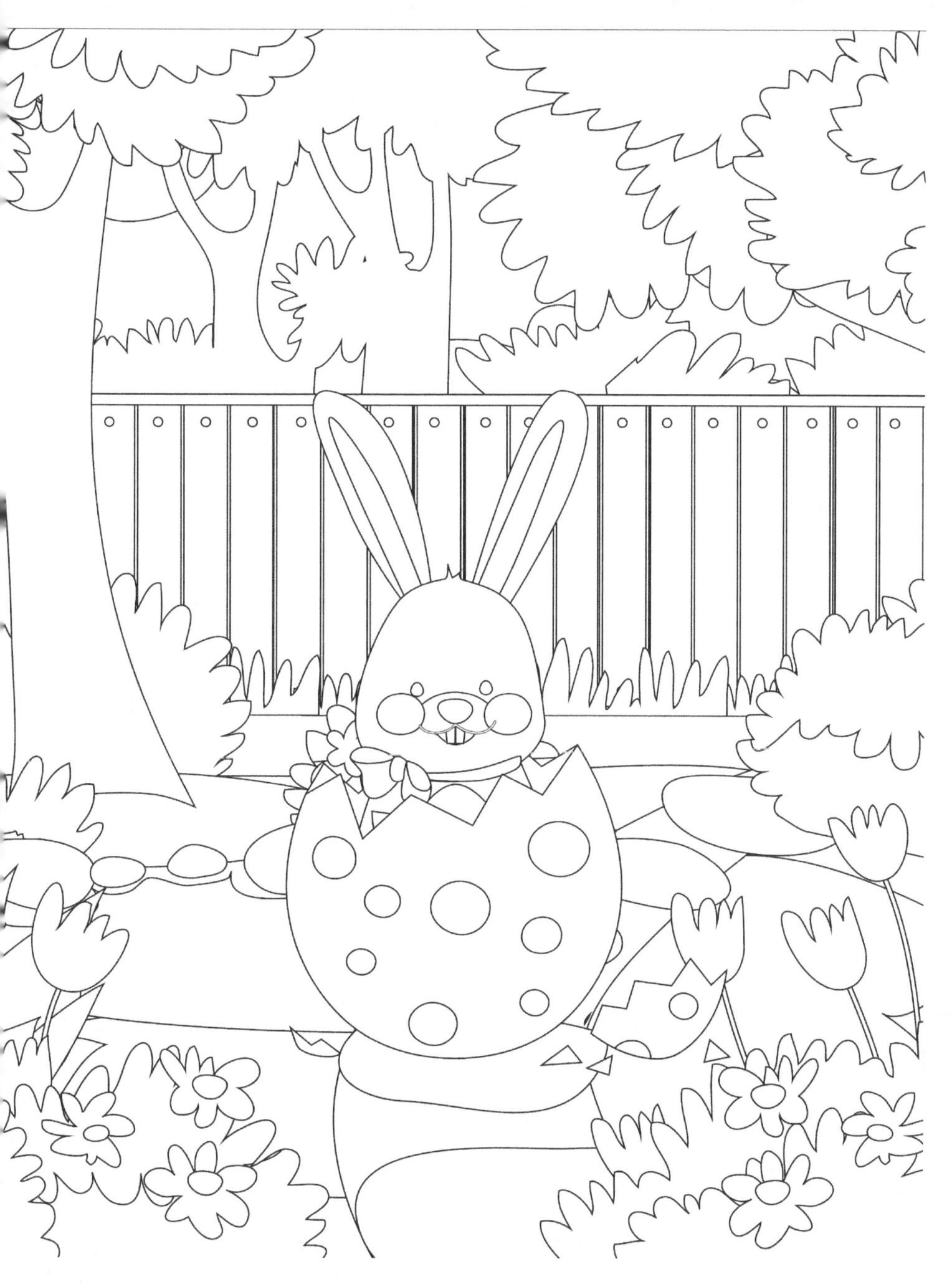

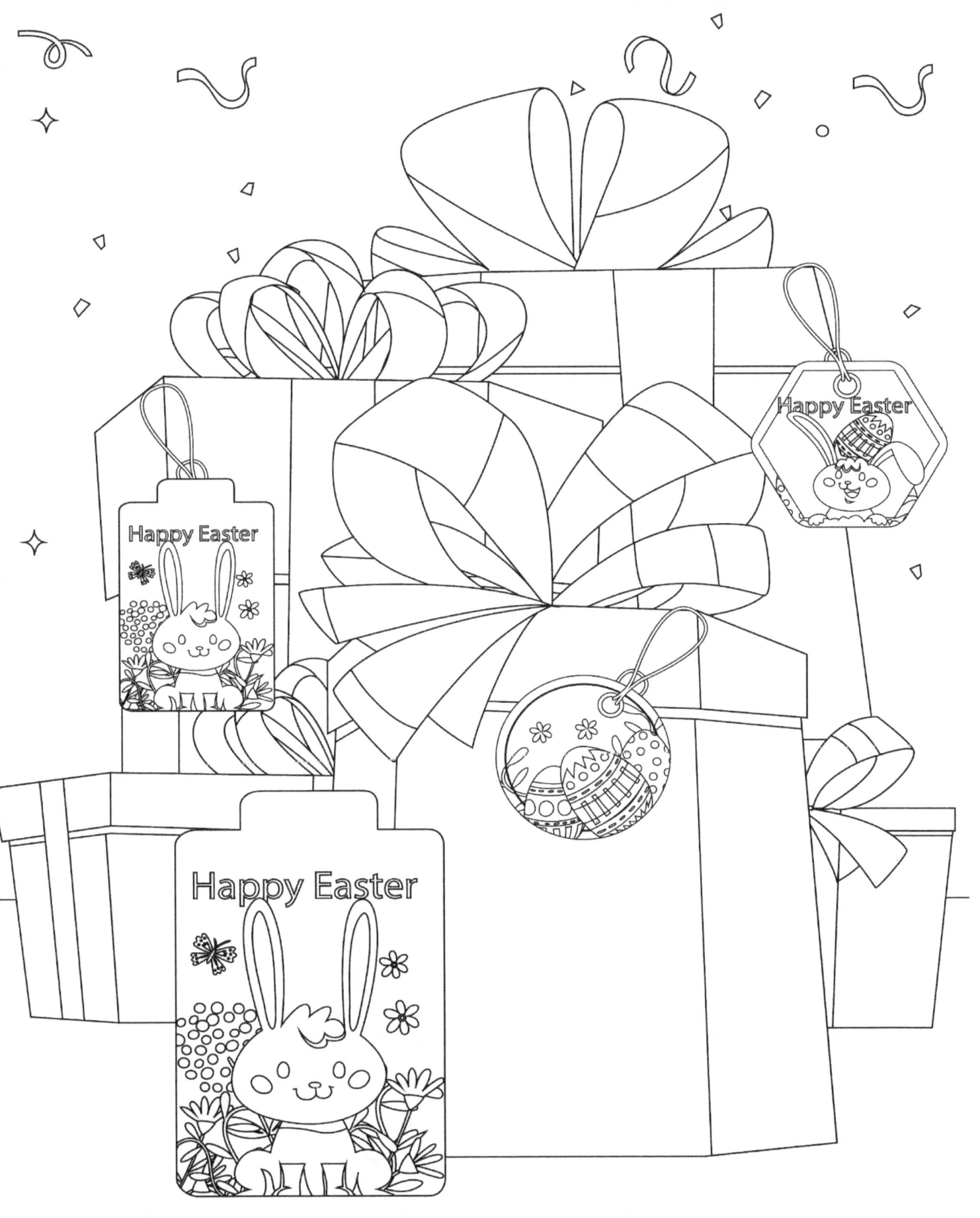

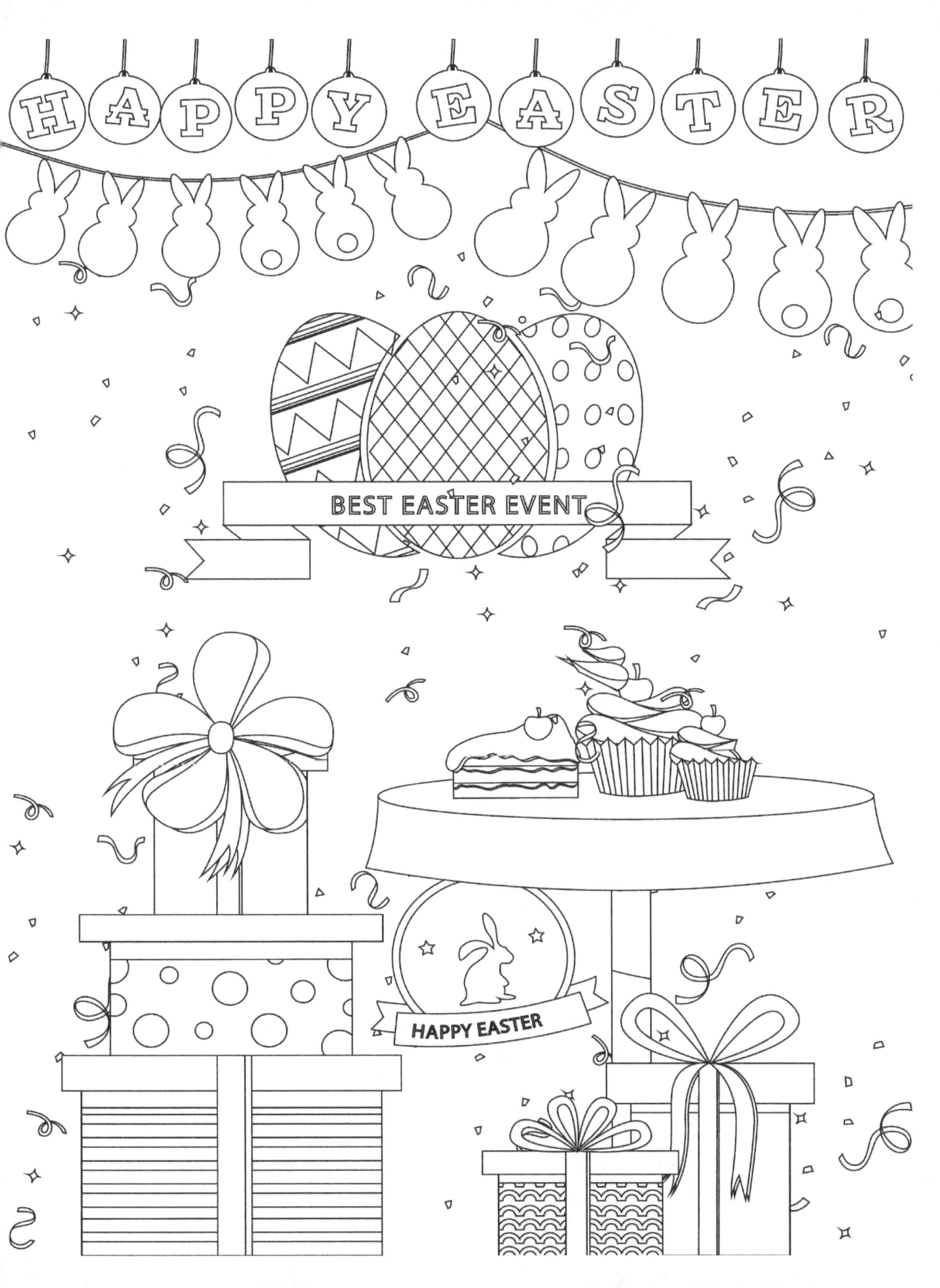

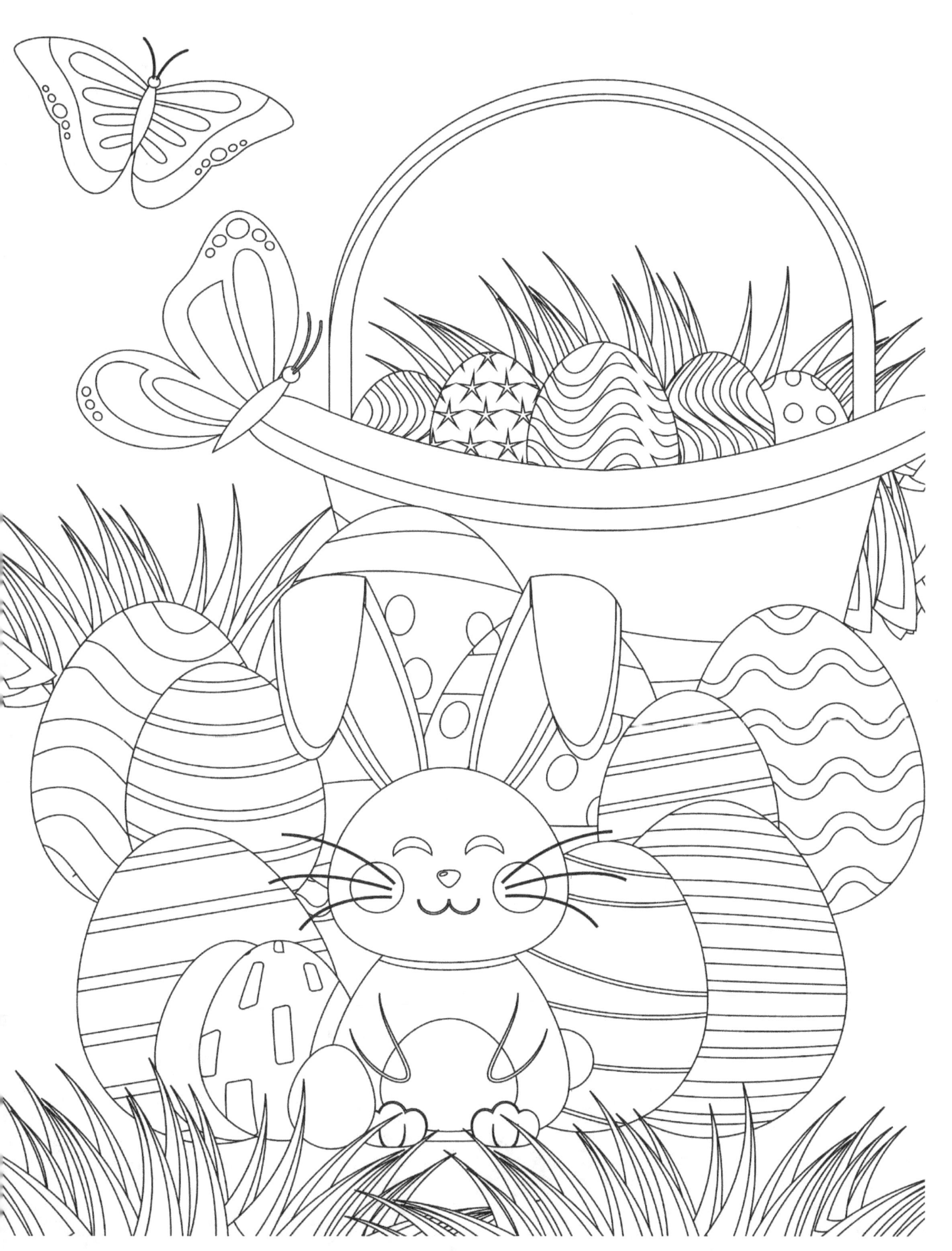

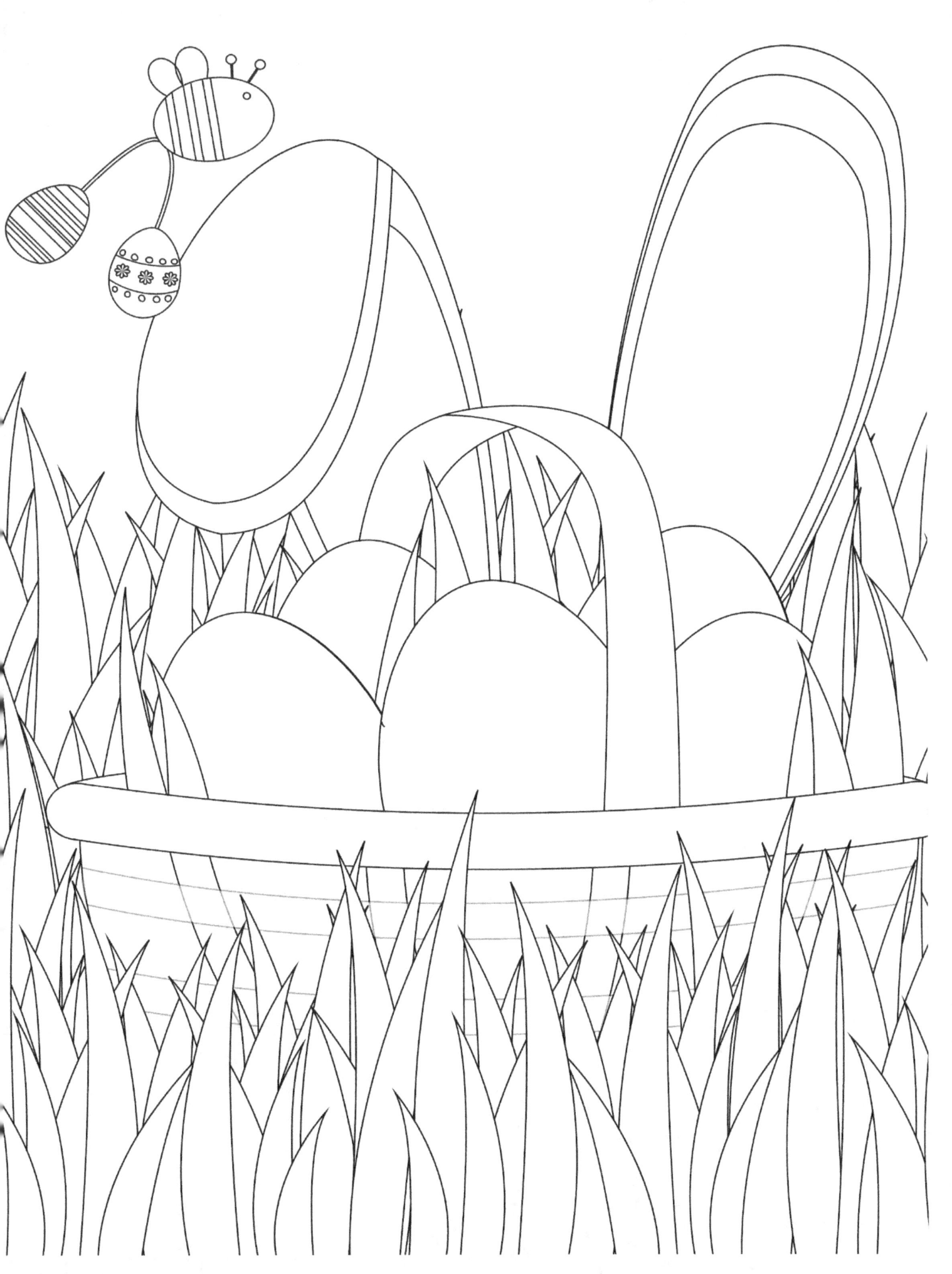

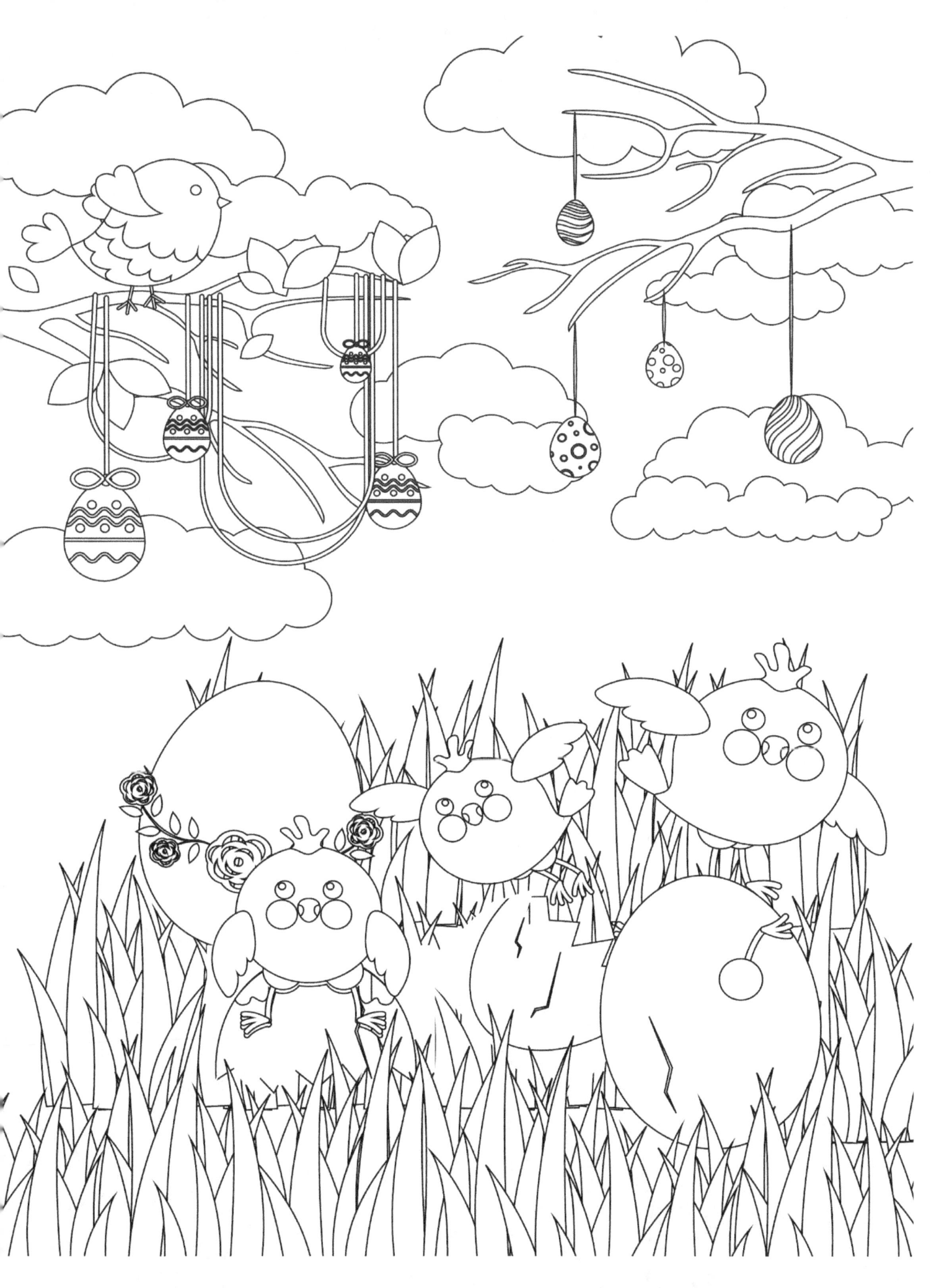

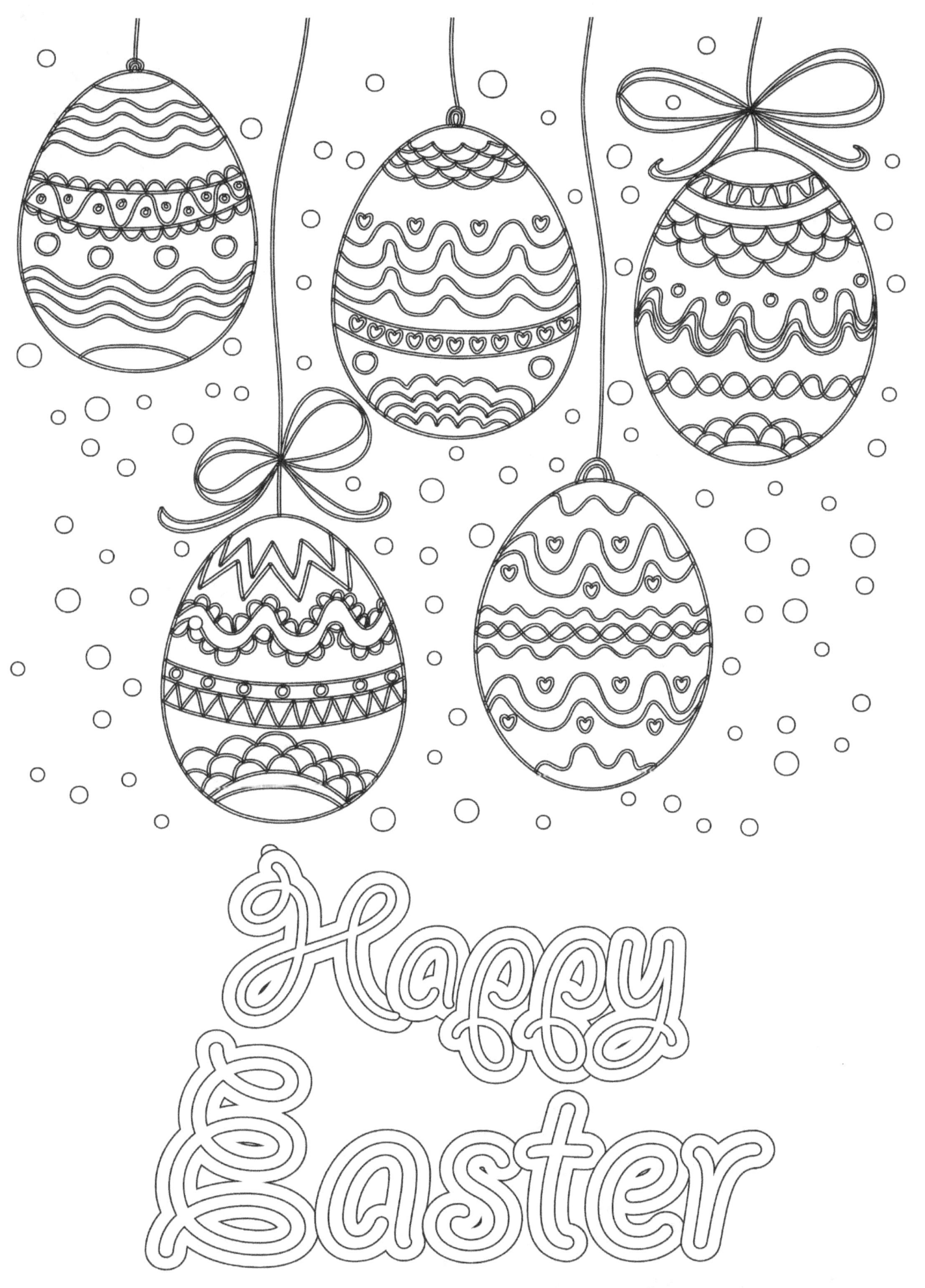

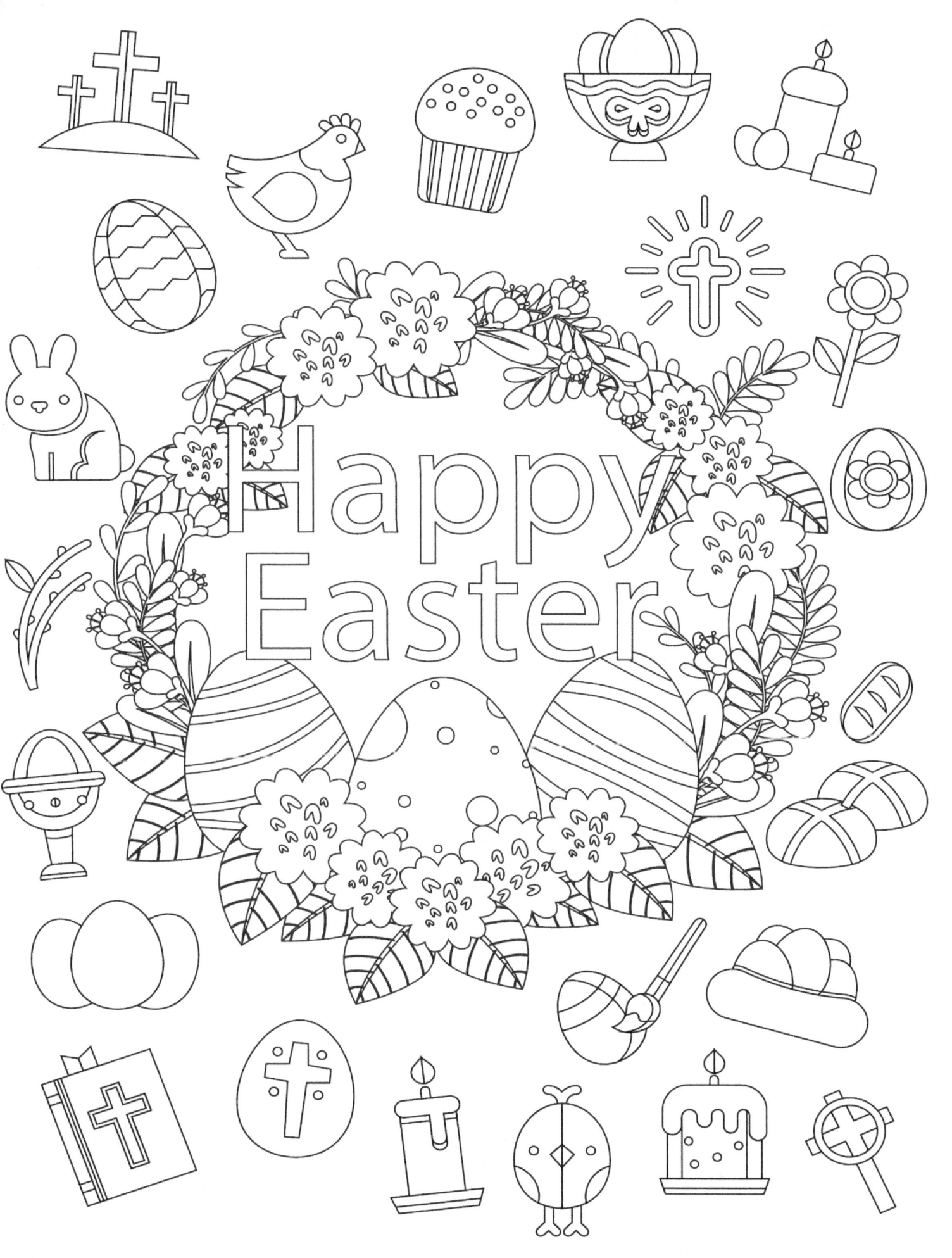

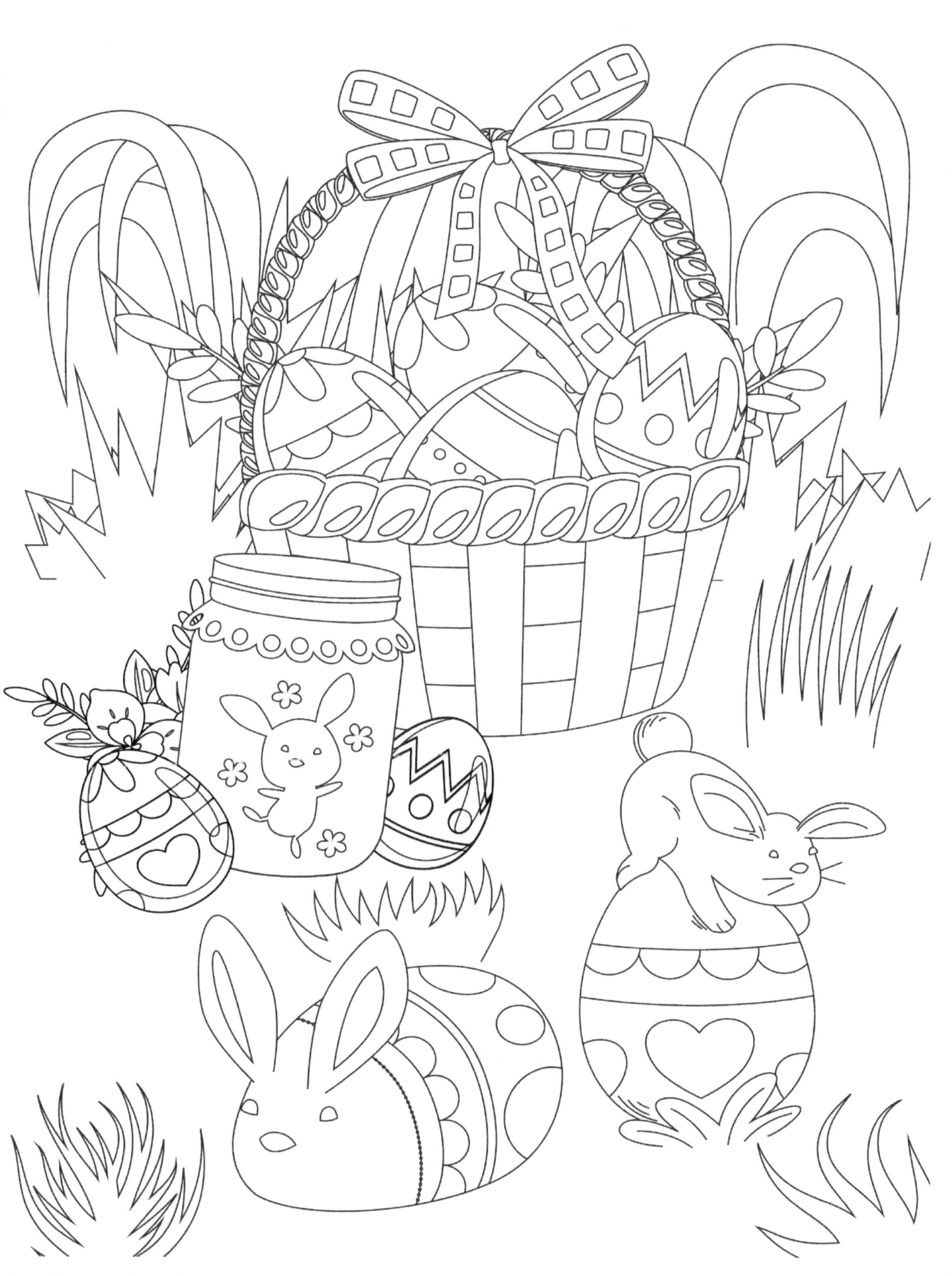

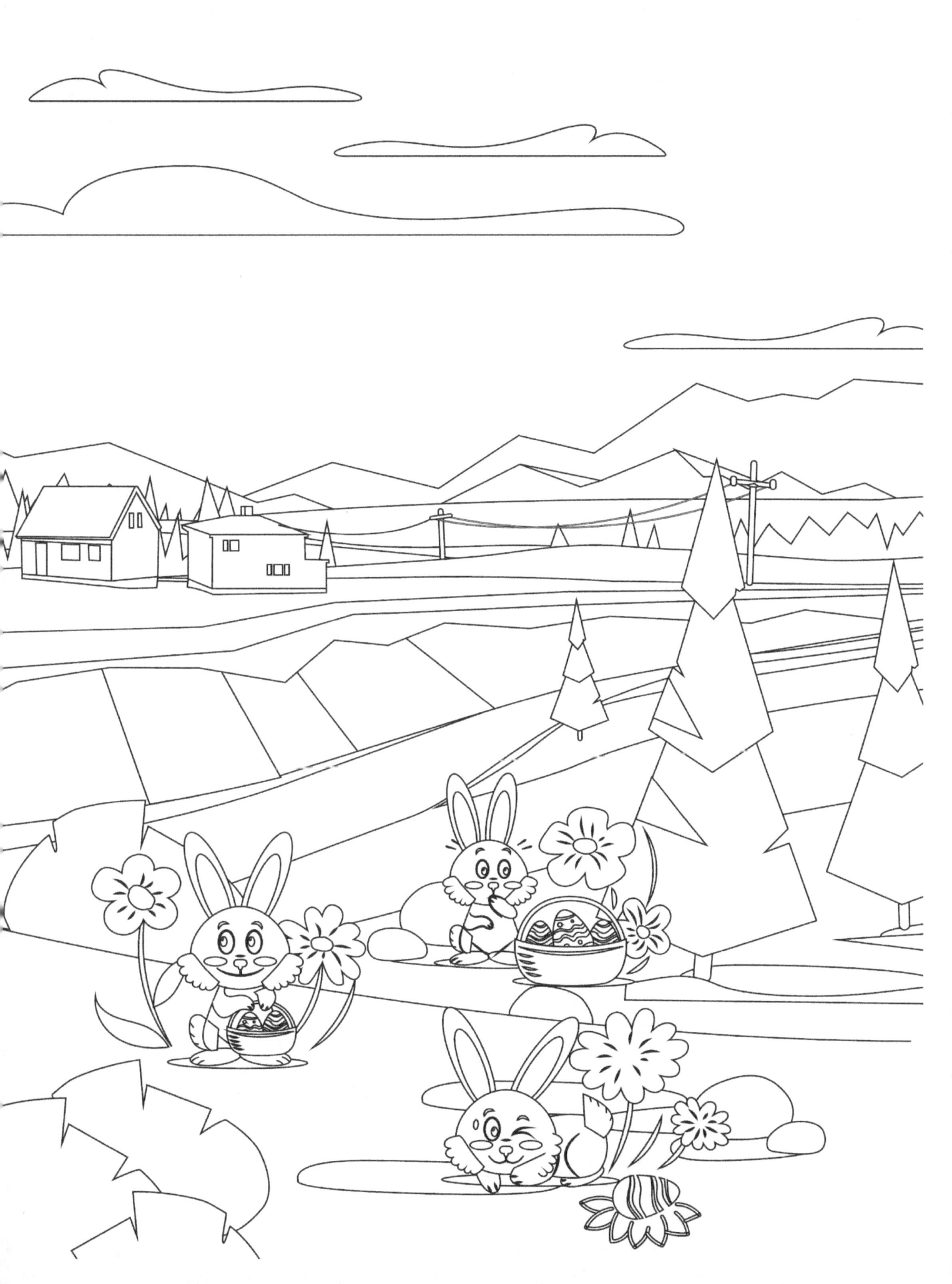

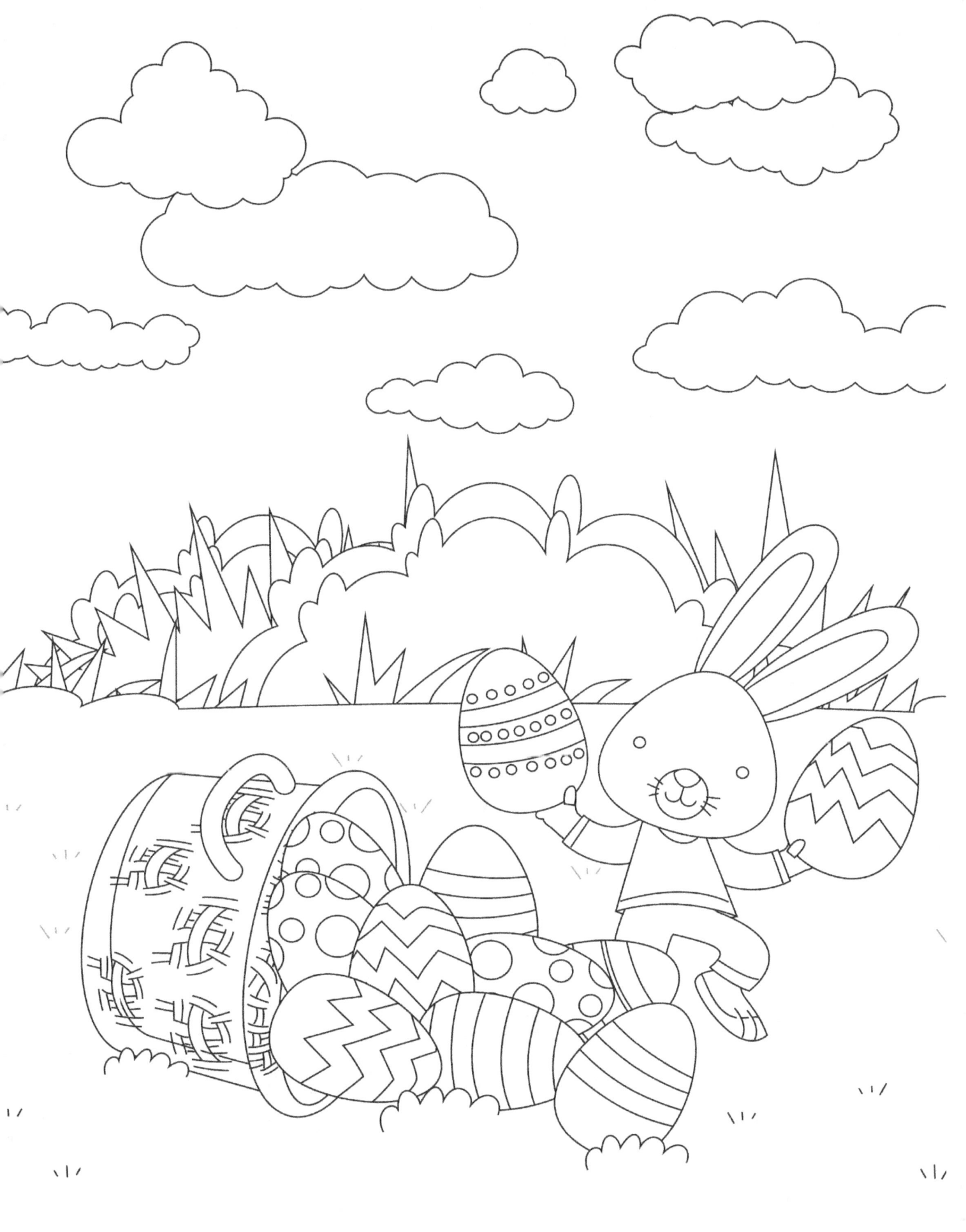

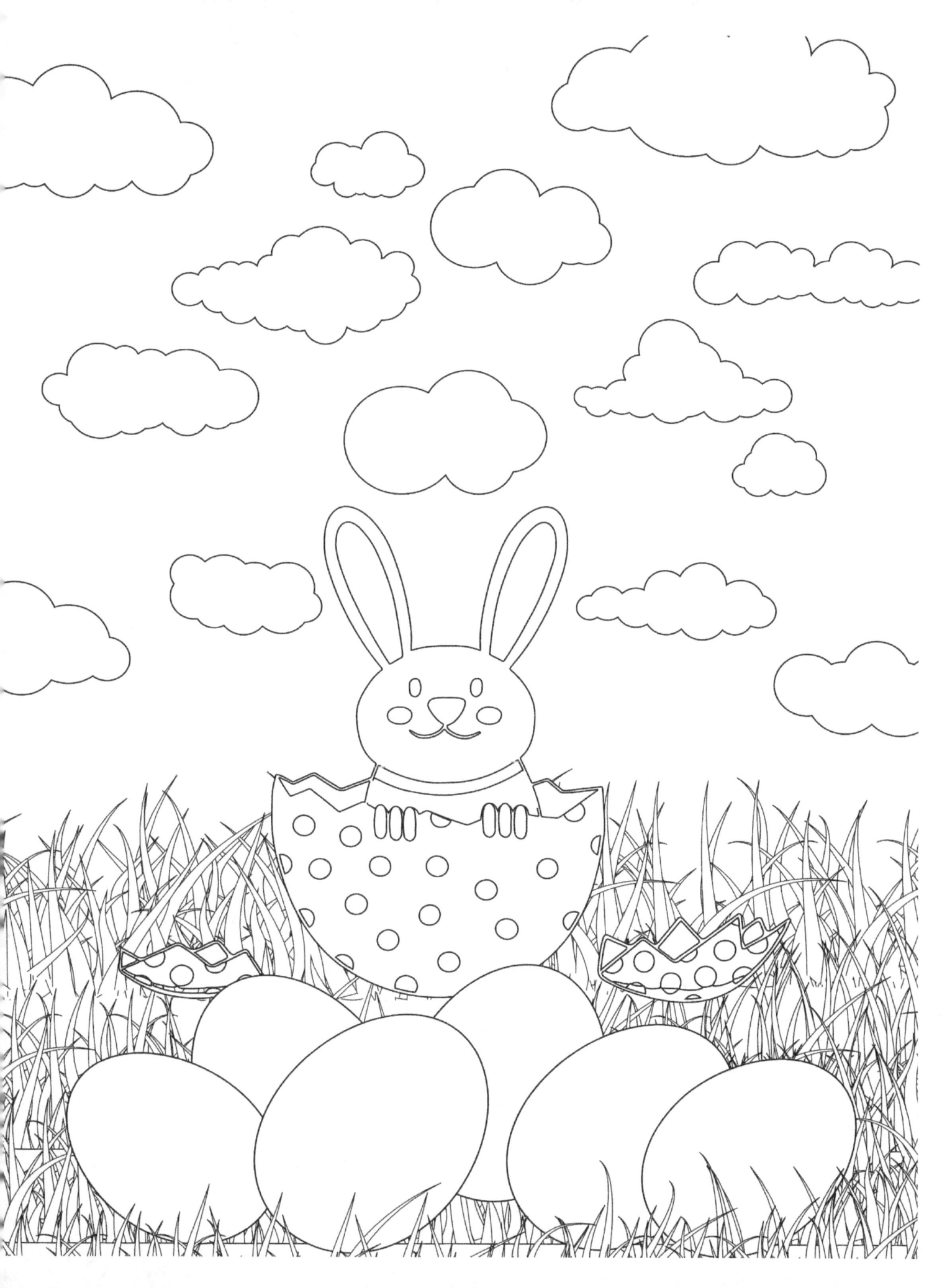

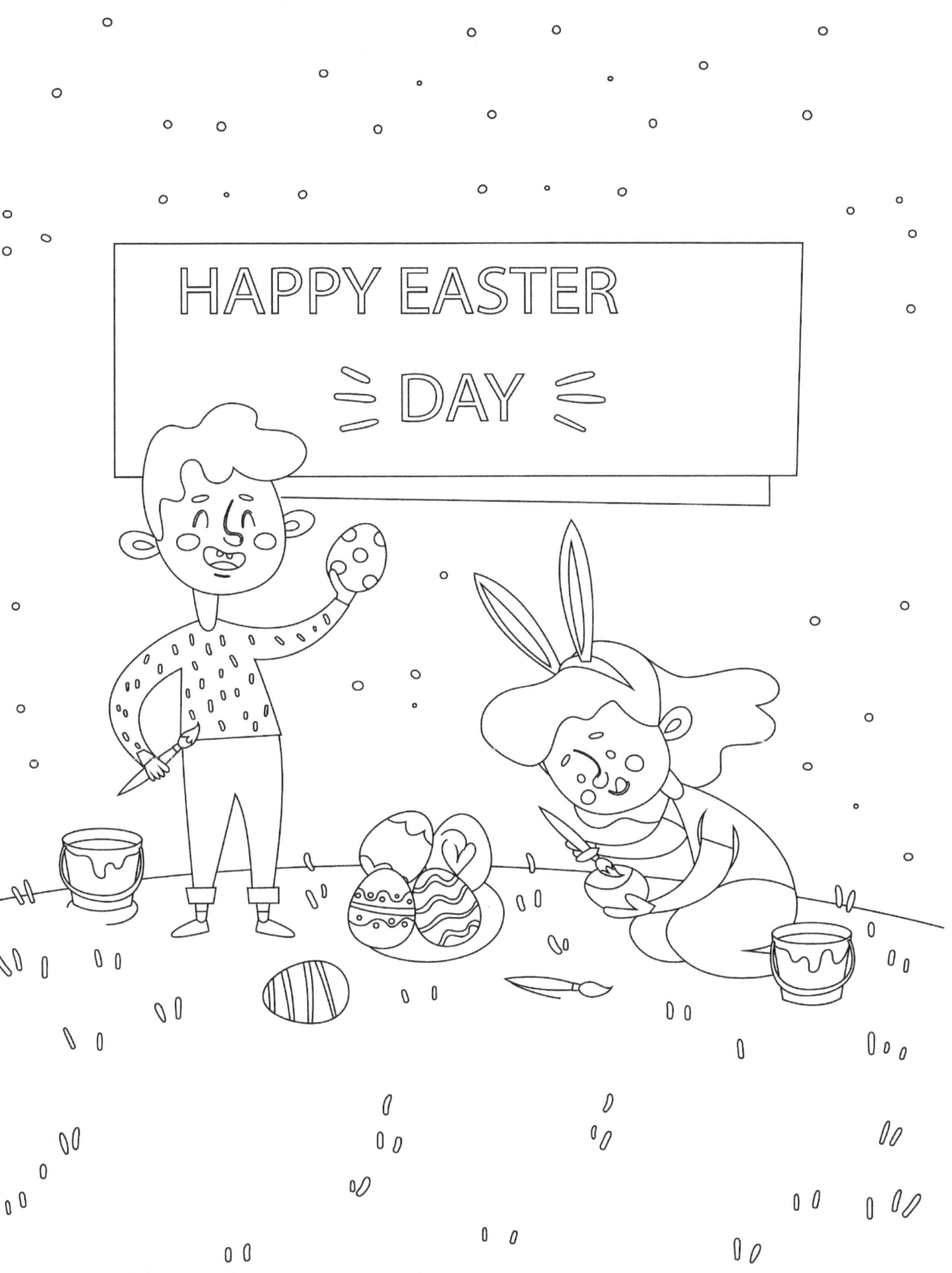

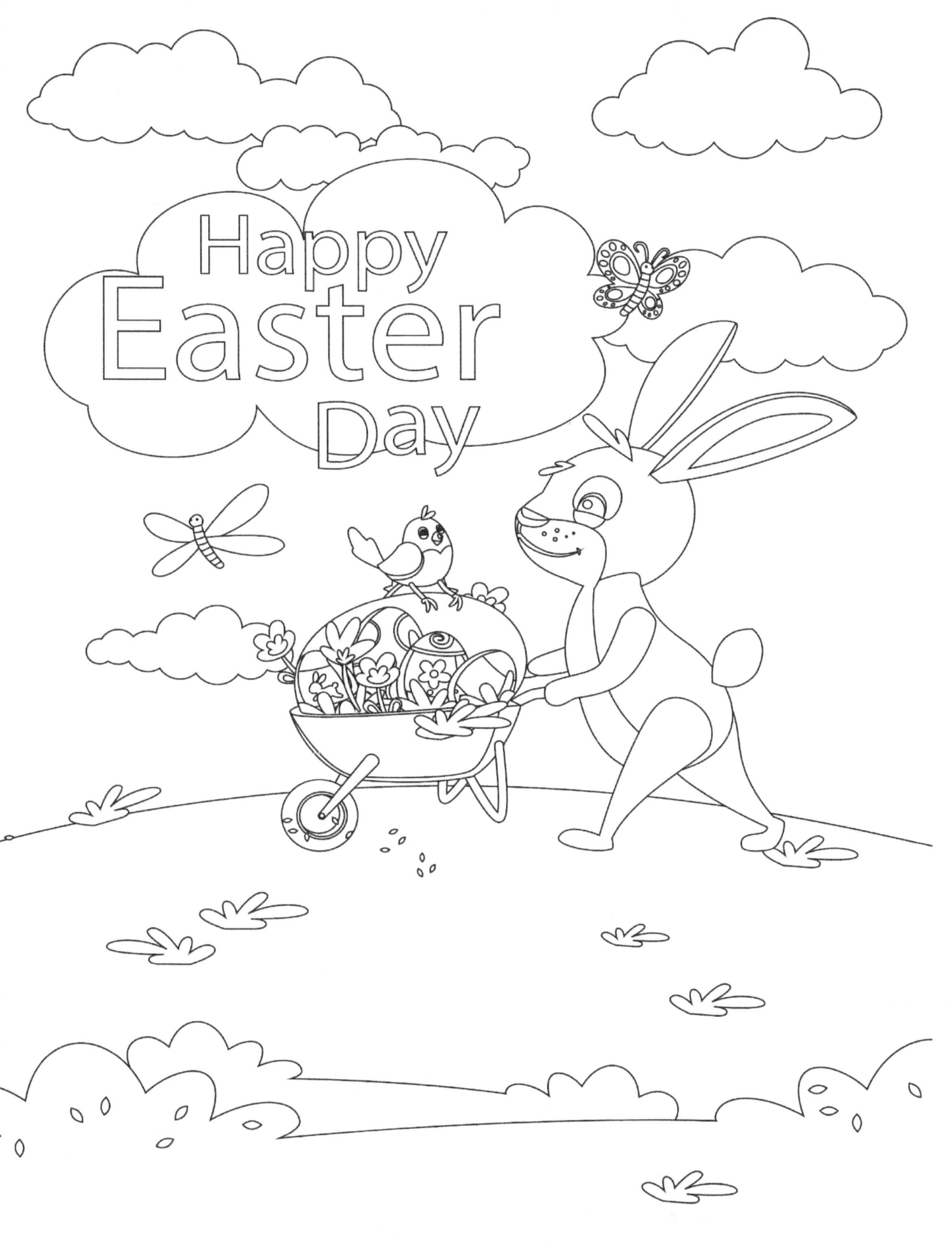

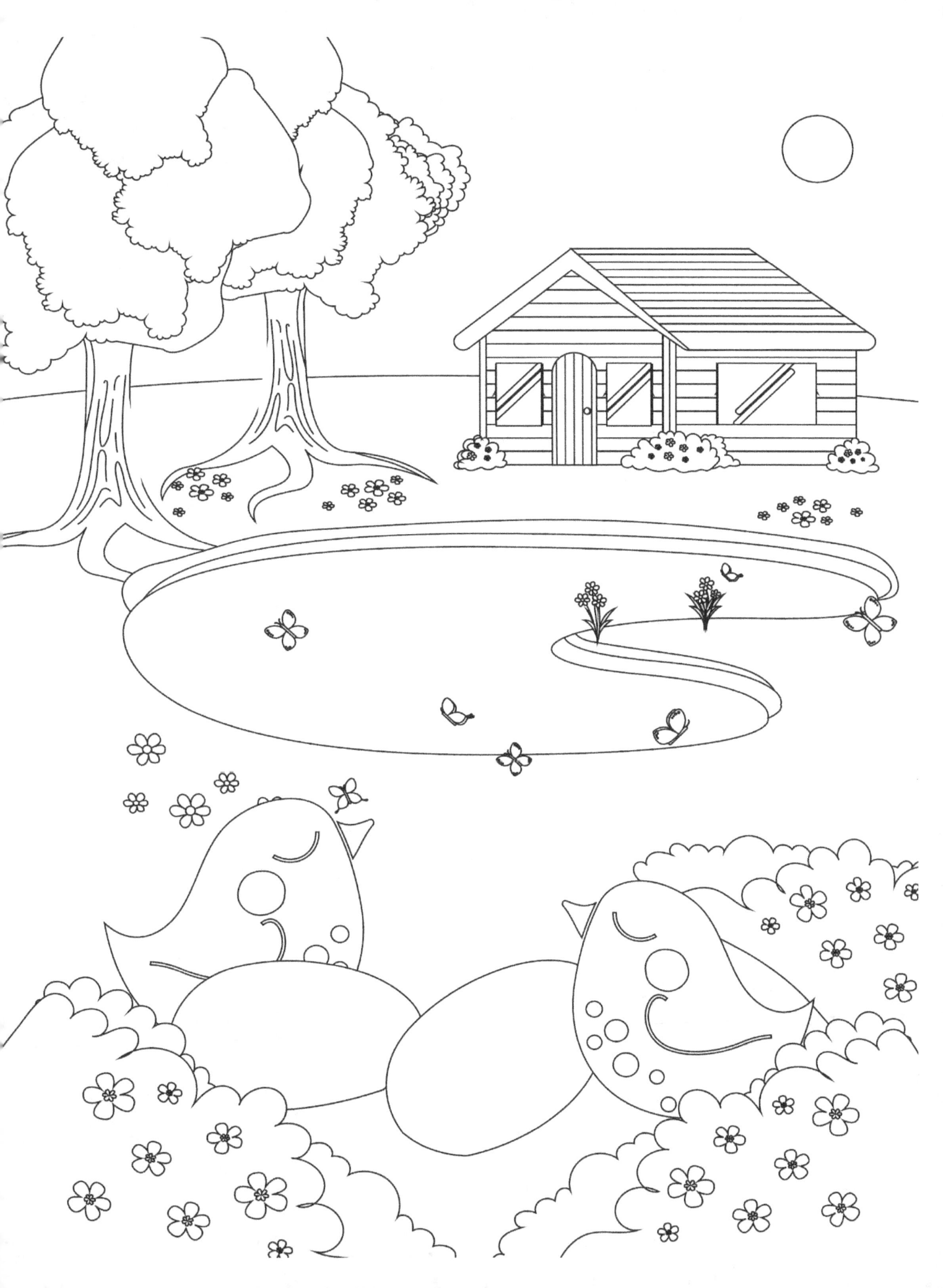

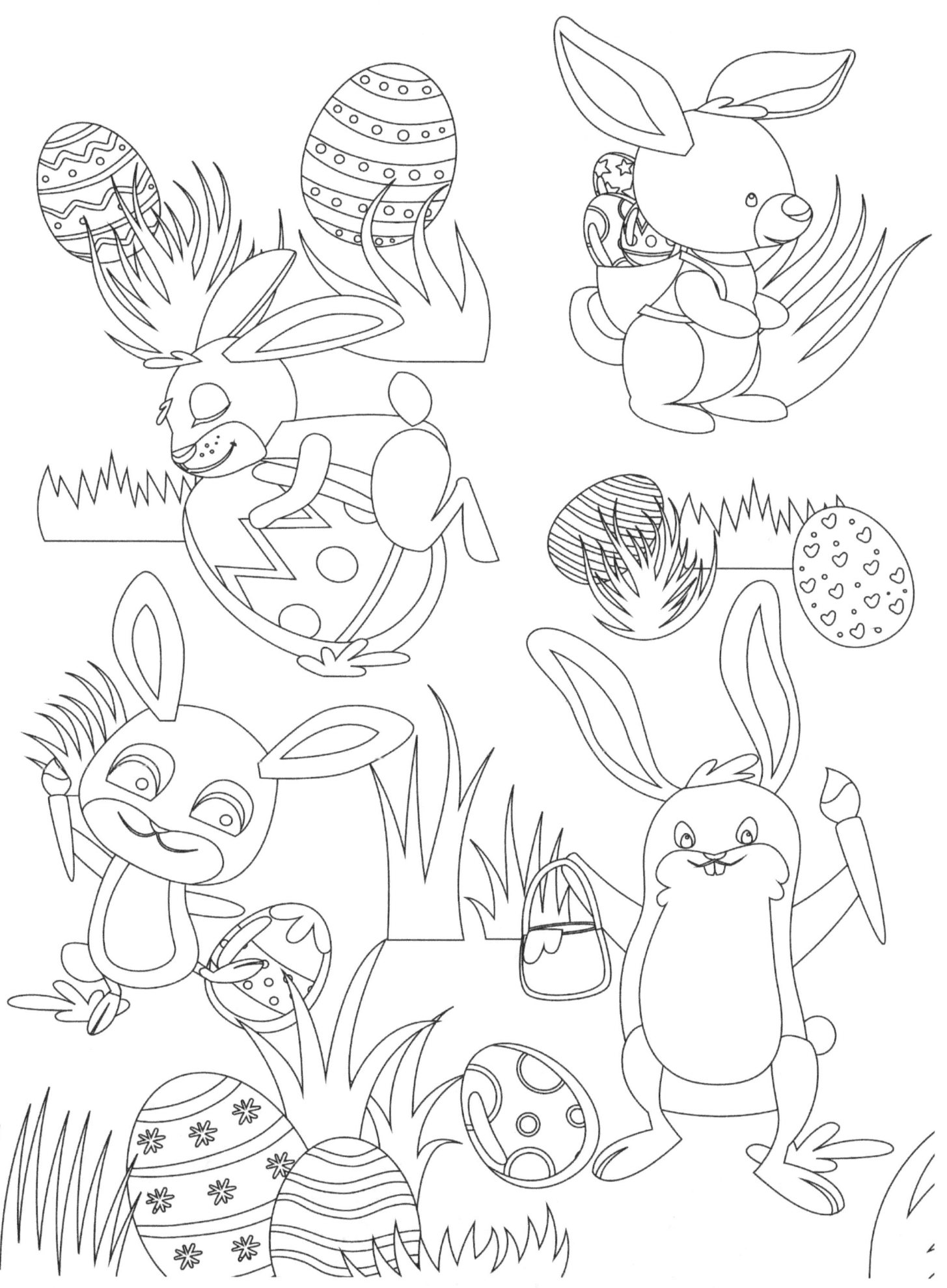

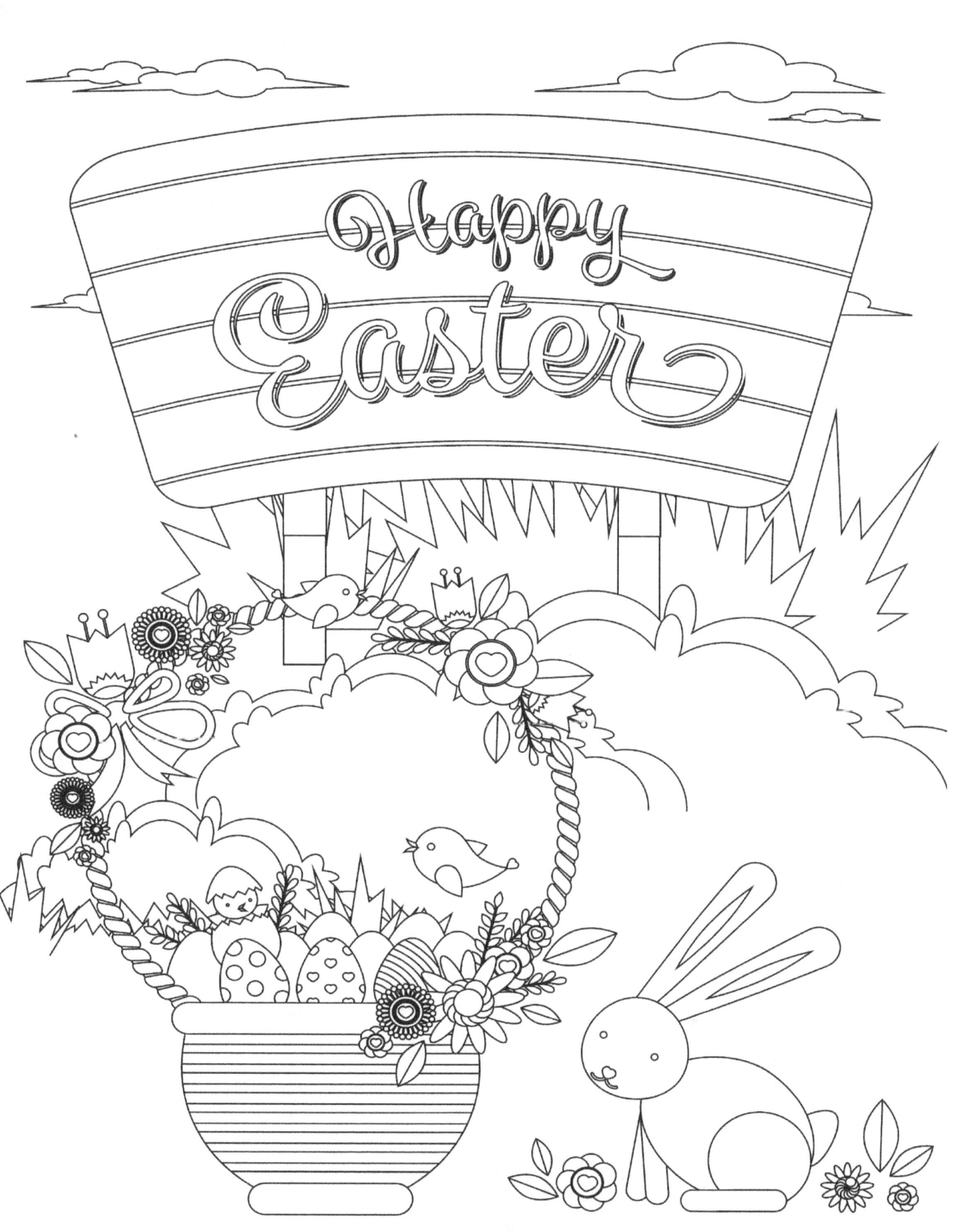

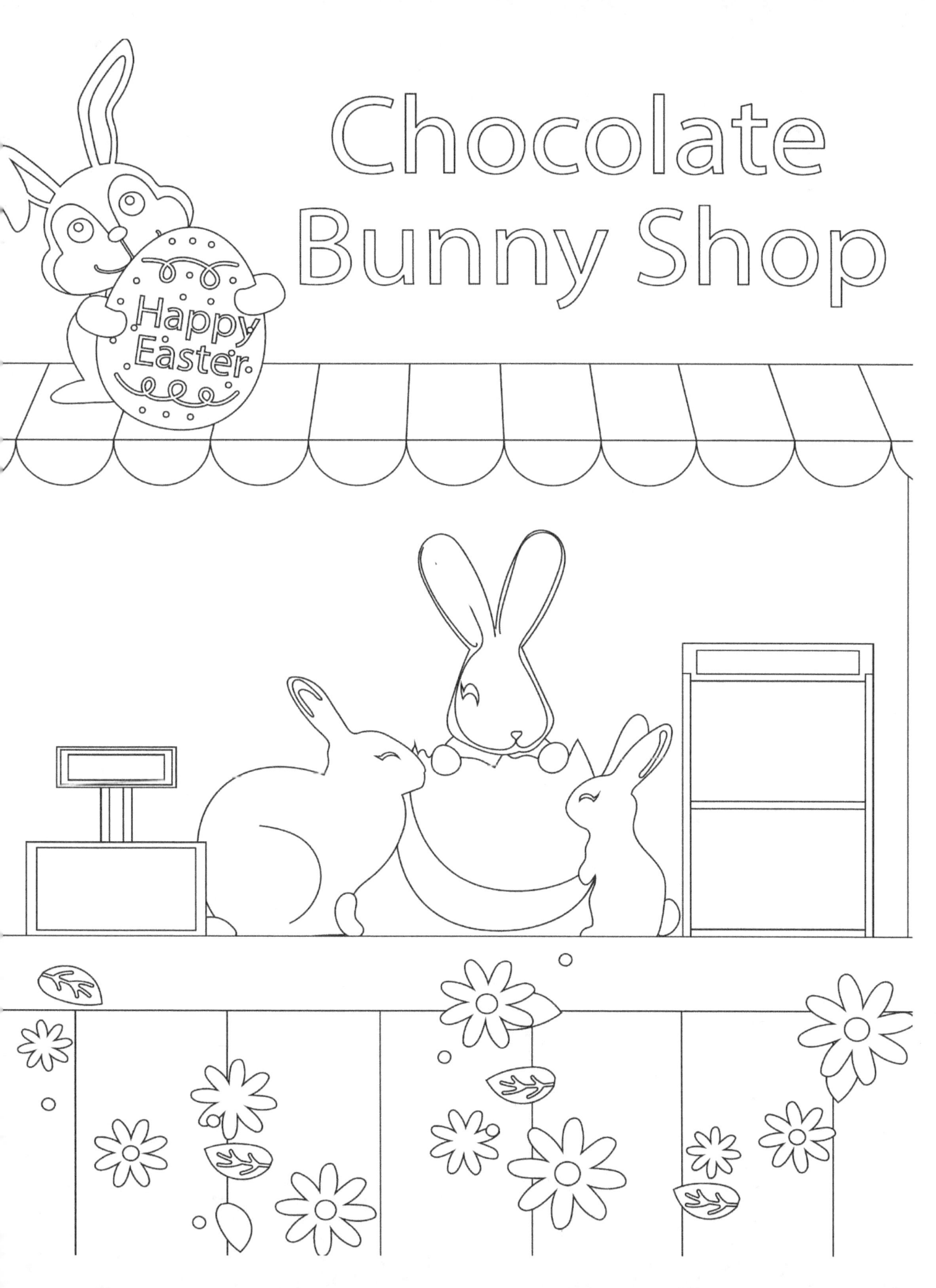

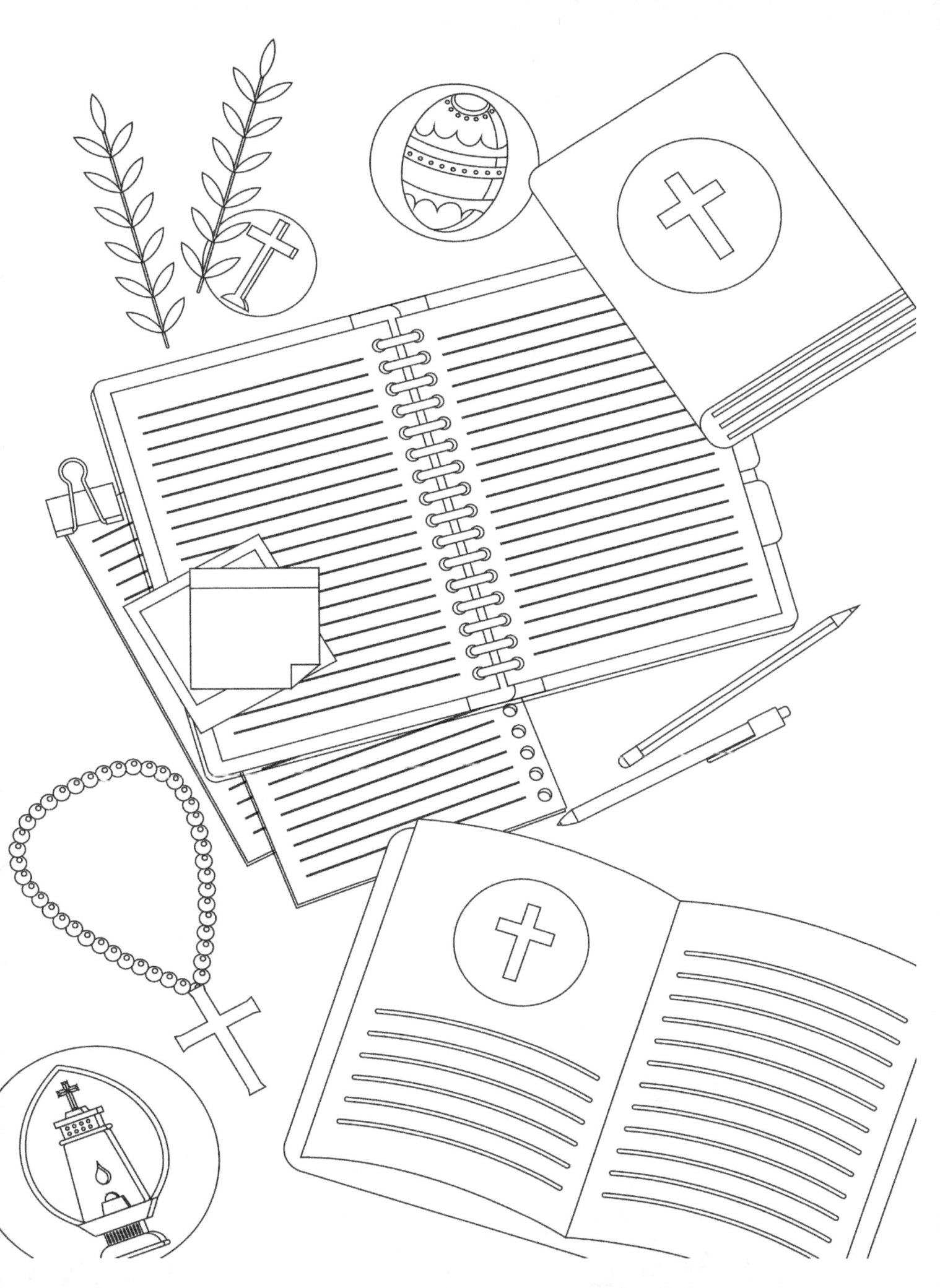

Easter Facts

1. Easter is the holiday where Christians remember the resurrection of Jesus. It's the oldest Christian holiday. It's also an important time for other religions too, and is often the same time as Passover.

2. The first chocolate egg to be produced and sold in the UK was made by Fry's of Bristol in 1873.

3. The world record for the tallest ever chocolate egg is 10.39 metres. It was made in Italy in 2011, and weighed 7,200 kg. That's more than an elephant!

4. The Easter tradition of a rabbit is thought to have originated in Germany, where it was originally a hare. A 16th century tale tells of how the Easter hare would visit children in the night and reward them for good behaviour.

5. The flower associated with Easter is the White Lilly. This is because it's the symbol of the resurrection.

6. Painting eggs is a popular activity around Easter and lets you get really creative. The name for this hobby is "Pysanka".

7. The Anglo-Saxon goddess, Eostre, is thought to be where the word Easter has come from.

8. 70% of sweet treats purchased around Easter are made with chocolate.

9. Most people think the first part of a chocolate bunny you should eat is the ear.

10. The first story that was published about a rabbit hiding eggs in a garden was written in 1680.

11. Each year, children in the UK receive on average 8.8 Easter eggs each. That's the equivalent of twice the recommended calorie intake they should have in a week.

12. Originally, Pretzels were associated with Easter because the twists were seen to represent people holding hands in prayer.

13. In America, more than 16 million jelly beans are consumed over Easter. They became a popular candy after manufacturers sent them to soldiers during the Civil War.

14. The largest ever Easter egg hunt was held in Florida in America. 501,000 eggs were hidden, with almost 10,000 children going to look for them.

15. Nearly 20 per cent of children have admitted to making themselves feel ill by eating too much chocolate at Easter.

16. There used to be a tradition where an egg throwing festival was held in churches. The priest would throw a hard boiled egg at one of the choir-boys, and they threw it between themselves. Whoever was holding it when the clock struck midnight was allowed to keep it.

17. Holy week, that leads up to Easter, includes Palm Sunday, Maundy Thursday, Good Friday, and Easter Sunday.

18. Easter isn't held on the same date every year, instead it's based on the position of the moon. It's celebrated on the first Sunday after the ecclesiastical full moon that occurs after March 21st.

19. Jesus wasn't the only person who came back to life on Easter Sunday, there were a number of other tombs that were found to be empty too.

20. The word Easter is only mentioned once in the Bible.

Easter Word Search

Can you find all of the hidden words?

```
K S T I N T W I Z K Z E G B M
R F J O C A F D W T D J C L W
B M F R H O L I D A Y N N U B
W X M G O K L T R F E V G O V
N R H E C X N A S U Z Y Y V T
J Z E I O E P H B Q M S S E O
M E H W L Z L A U S O R I G S
H C G D A F F O D I L S M G B
N F H O T C R O S S B U N S T
K E T K E B O T A U D I E B K
P V A B N Z W A N Y L X L H N
O Q V R N F A L P K G G C Z H
V V J P O Y L C C P G E A T I
D V X B B S E U O J W J K C B
L P T R W S D A T P K K E P V
```

Bonnet	Daffodils	Hot Cross Buns
Bunny	Ducklings	Lent
Chick	Eggs	Parade
Chocolate	Holiday	Simnel Cake

Easter Quiz

1. What's the most popular sweet treat to give, and eat, at Easter?
2. Which flower is most associated with Easter?
3. Easter celebrates the resurrection of who?
4. What is the name of the Thursday before Easter?
5. Easter is the second most popular holiday for purchasing sweets, what is the most popular?
6. How many days after his death did Jesus come back to life?
7. Easter baskets were originally designed to look like which places that you often find eggs?
8. Easter is celebrated in December of every year. TRUE or FALSE?
9. The ancient Egyptians and Persians saw eggs as a symbol for what?
10. The tradition of egg painting goes back to Simon of Cyrene, who put down his egg basket to help Jesus do what?
11. In America, more than 700 million peeps are sold, and eaten, each year at Easter. What are they made from?
12. Who betrayed Jesus?
13. What is the name for the period of fasting that leads up to Easter?
14. Simnel Cakes, which are eaten on Easter Sunday, were traditionally made on which day?
15. Which famous American building hosts an egg hunt every year at Easter?
16. Which of these is not a popular Easter Symbol? Cross, Eggs, Cats, Rabbits
17. You'll get good luck if you wear new what at Easter?
18. Where does the Easter Bunny hide eggs for children to search for them?
19. What's the name of the sweet rolls with raising that people eat at Easter?
20. On the island of Bermuda, what to residents fly in the sky on Good Friday?

Easter Crossword

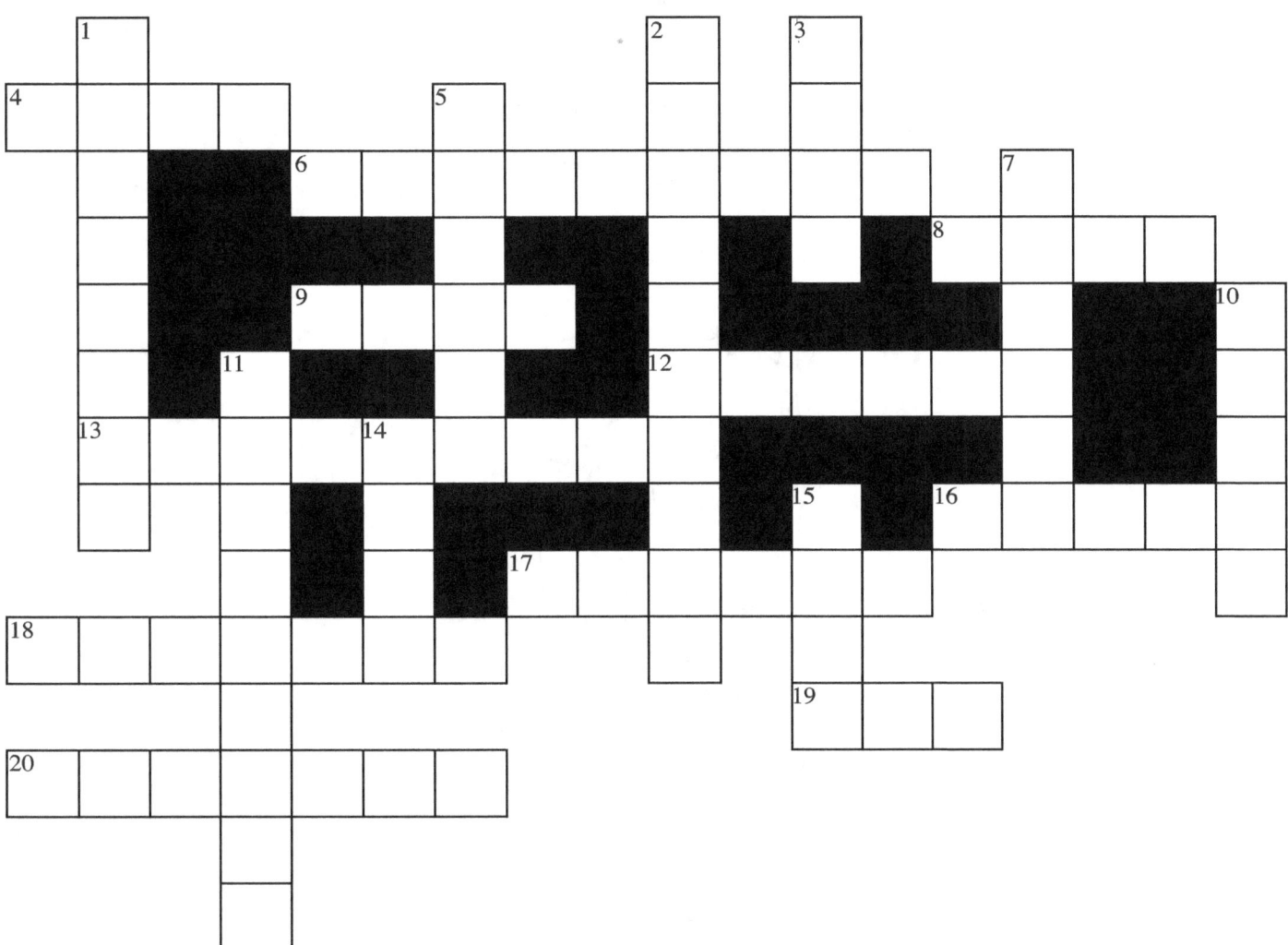

Across

4. Which heavenly body decides which date Easter is held each year? (4)
6. The official flower of Easter (5, 4)
8. _____ Friday, two days before Easter (4)
9. The period of fasting that takes place before Easter (4)
12. The type of hat traditionally worn at Easter (6)
13. What are the eggs given on Easter made from? (9)
16. Easter celebrates the resurrection of who? (5)
17. The day of the week that Easter is always celebrated on (6)
18. Which twisted baked good was originally associated with Easter? (7)
19. The part of a chocolate bunny that most people like to eat first (3)
20. The tradition of painting eggs for Easter (7)

Down

1. Wearing new clothing on Easter is said to bring what in the year to come? (4, 4)
2. In America, more than 16 million of which sweet are eaten at Easter? (5, 5)
3. _____ Sunday, the beginning of Easter Week (4)
5. The type of cake usually eaten on Easter (6)
7. The word Easter is derived from the name of which Anglo-Saxon goddess? (6)
10. Hot _____ Buns (5)
11. The Traditional meat served on Easter (5, 4)
14. The number of times the word "Easter" is mentioned in the Bible (4)
15. The Easter bunny was originally, in German, which similar animal? (4)

Spot The Difference

6 Differences to Spot. Can You Spot Them All?

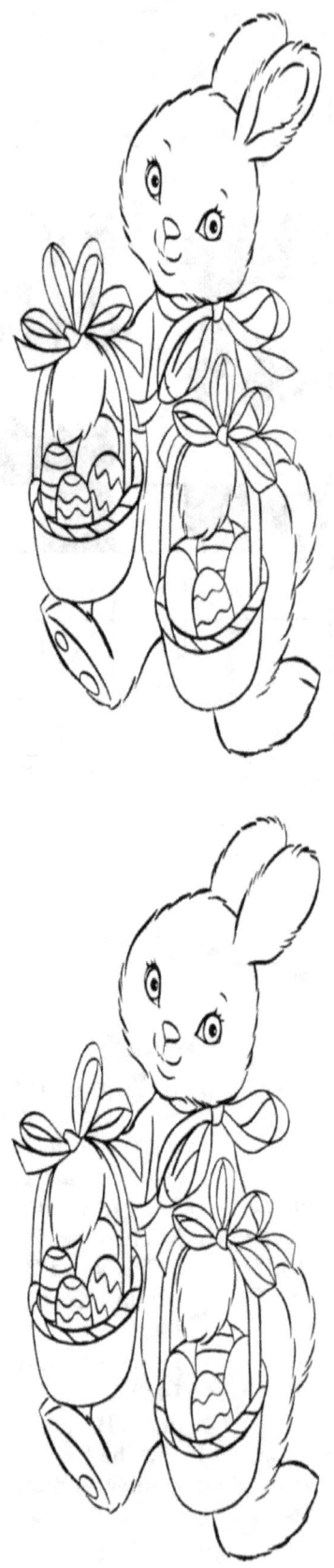

Answers

1. Chocolate
2. The White Lily
3. Jesus
4. Maundy Thursday
5. Halloween
6. Three
7. Bird's Nests
8. FALSE
9. Life
10. Carry his Cross
11. Marshmallow
12. Judas Iscariot
13. Lent
14. Mothering Sunday
15. The White House
16. Cats
17. Clothes
18. In the Garden
19. Hot Cross Buns
20. Kites

Spot The Difference

1. Left Ear
2. Ribbon Around the Neck
3. Left Foot
4. Right Foot
5. Bow ont he Right Basket
6. Right Eyebrow

Thank you for purchasing this book.

If you would like to know more about Aryla Publishing Books please visit:-

www.ArylaPublishing.com

Or follow us on
Facebook
Twitter
Instagram
for *free promotions*

@arylapublishing

We would love to know what you think of this book so please leave us a review.

Have a wonderful day ☺

Other Coloring Books from Aryla Publishing

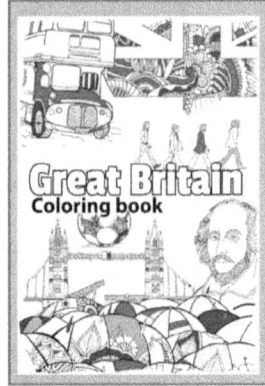
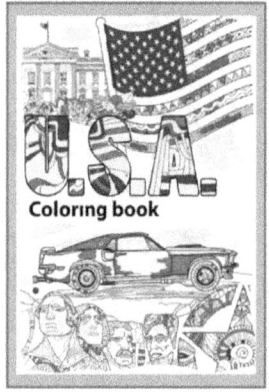
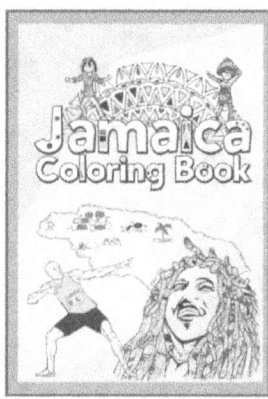
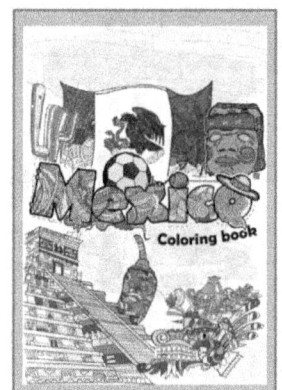

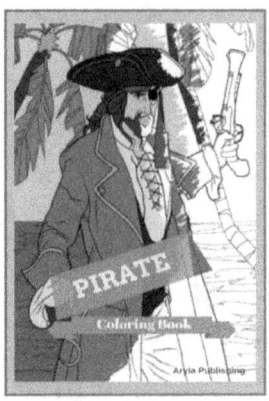
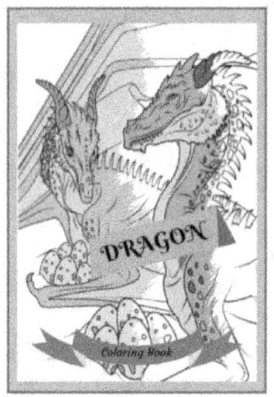
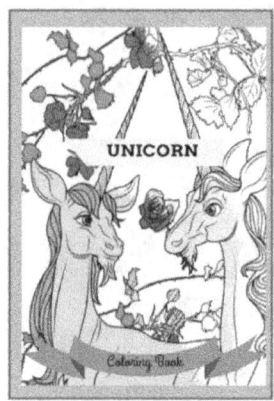
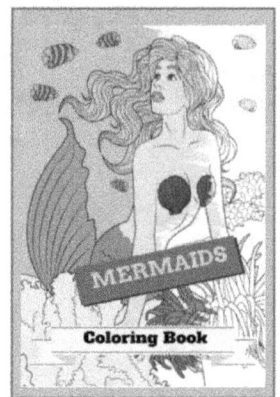

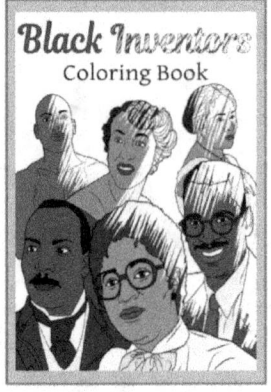
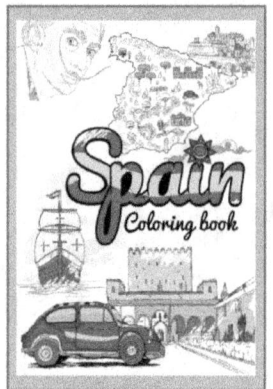
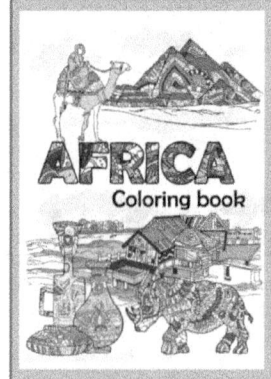
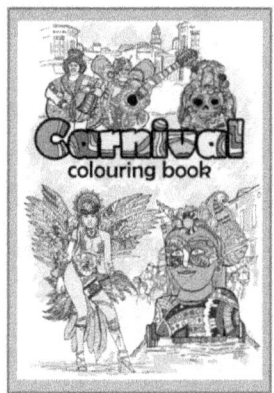

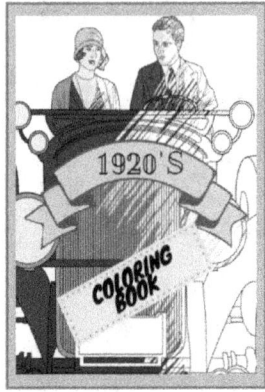
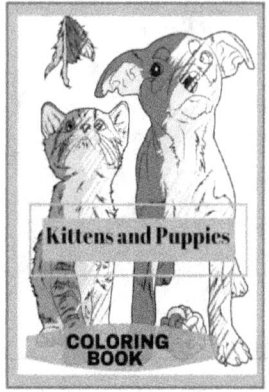
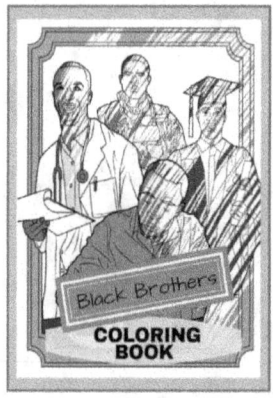
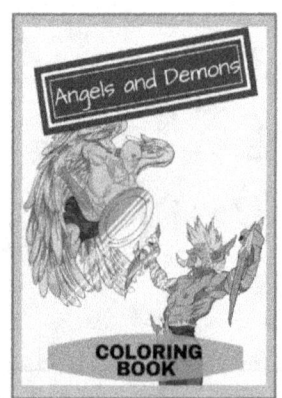

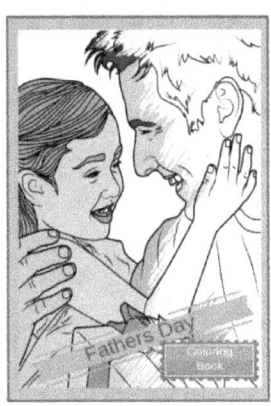
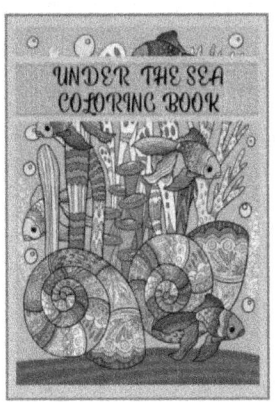
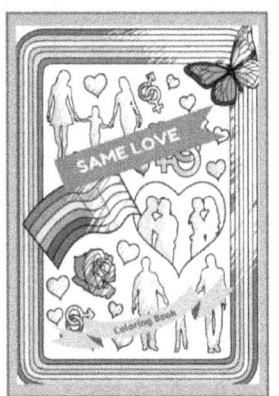
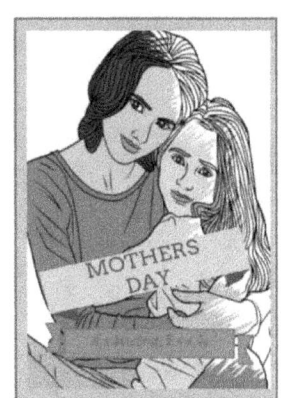
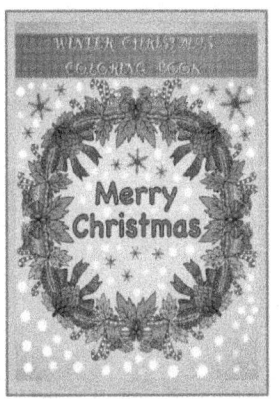
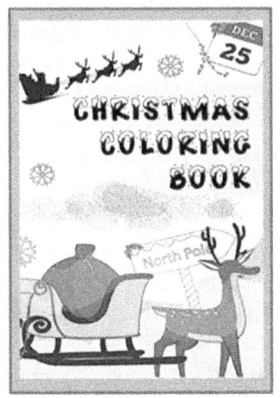
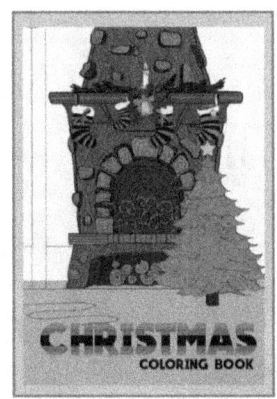
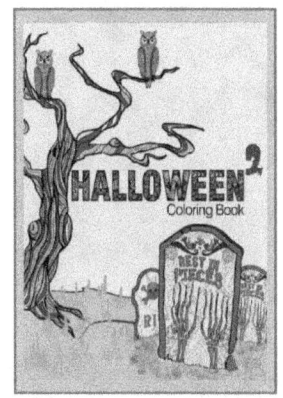
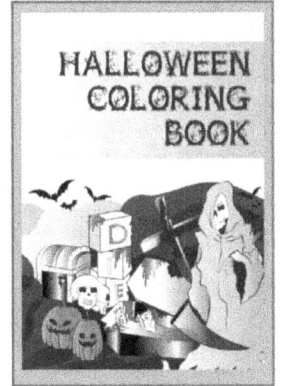
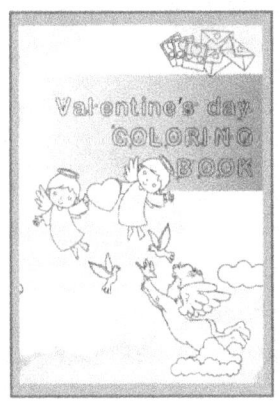
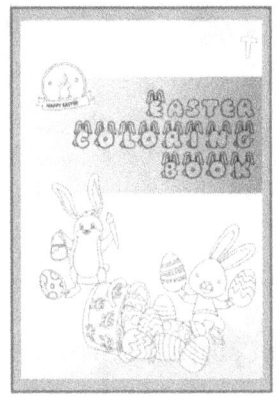
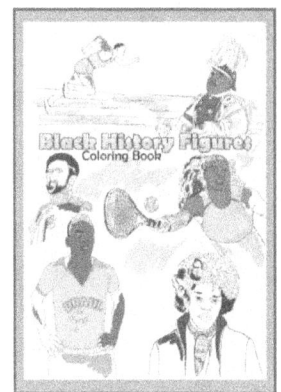

Visit **www.ArylaPublishing.com**
to find out about all new releases.

Follow us @arylapublishing on Twitter Instagram & Facebook

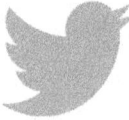  

Search for Aryla Publishing on

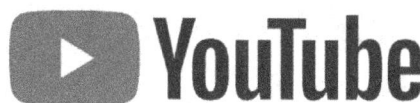 YouTube

Check out our <u>Book Trailers</u>

<u>Subscribe</u> **to keep up to date with new releases!**

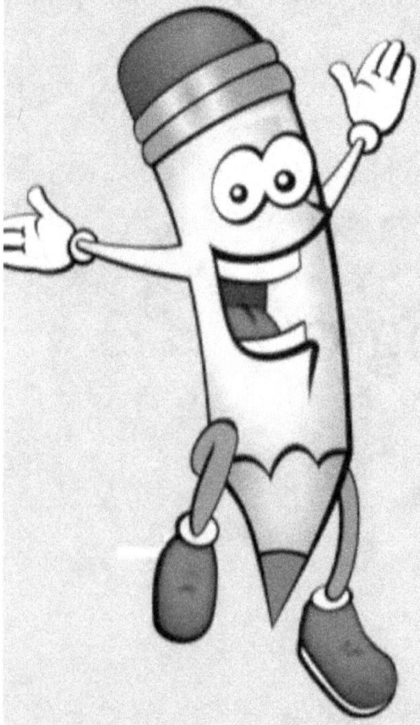

WE WOULD LOVE YOUR FEEDBACK

PLEASE LEAVE REVIEW AT:-

www.amazon.com/gp/product-review/1912675013

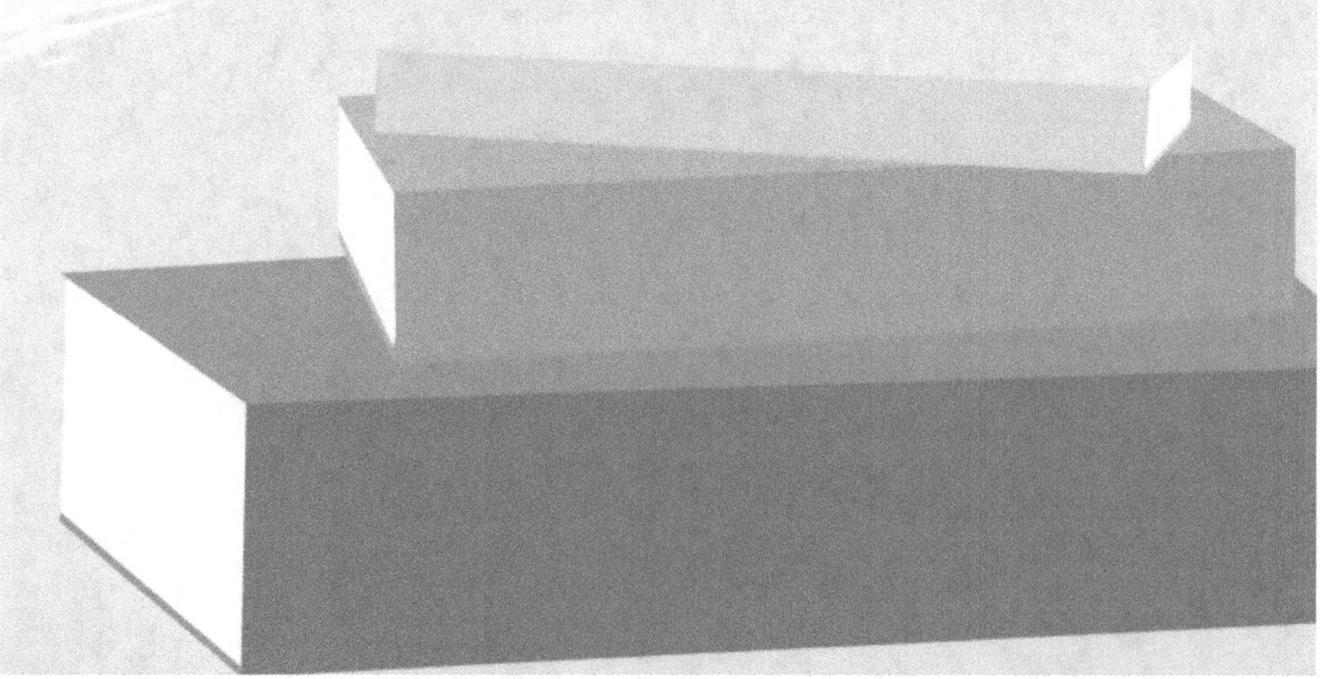

www.ingramcontent.com/pod-product-compliance
Lightning Source LLC
Chambersburg PA
CBHW081627220526
45468CB00009B/2337